T0146936

Through the Cracks
The Magic in Me

TRISH AVERY

BALBOA.
PRESS

A DIVISION OF HAY HOUSE

Balboa Press books may be ordered through booksellers or by contacting:

Balboa Press
A Division of Hay House
1663 Liberty Drive
Bloomington, IN 47403
www.balboapress.com
1 (877) 407-4847

Print information available on the last page.

ISBN: 978-1-5043-8747-7 (sc)
ISBN: 978-1-5043-8748-4 (hc)
ISBN: 978-1-5043-8791-0 (e)

Library of Congress Control Number: 2017913849

Balboa Press rev. date: 09/11/2017

Introduction

Trish was born in the 1960's where compared to today life was simpler and kids were kids and were to be seen and not heard.

This book is a true account of a young girl born to a mother who had no domestic skills. Her mother had many children and sooner or later most of them ended up in the child care system from neglect and abuse.

Trish was born knowing who she was at a young age. She came to this world with abilities all of us who are born into this world have but due to free will are mainstreamed and soon forget of these abilities. Trish was not mainstreamed and her abilities were used for survival. The touch of one's hand told her if she could trust, astral traveling gave her the escape, and speaking with spirits gave her comfort of friends.

When she was taken away and put into the child care system at the age of 4.the world became tough and scary. Trish was no longer in the closet she spent most of her time, she had never been beyond that house she lived in.

Trish would soon find out that who she was, was different than the world outside of her house.

Trish went through her childhood going from home to

home trying to find where she belonged. She was different in a world full of labels.

Her story takes you on a journey finding herself through, drama, death, judgement and love. As her abilities enhance and she becomes the woman she is today.

Trish teaches us that being true to who we are is the most important thing in life and that being different and embracing it has reward beyond imaginable.

Trish has never let the opinions of others define her and looked at every obstacle as a challenge. Helping people with her abilities along the way and sending peace and love in this world and beyond.

Trish's message is "Do not let others make you feel different, just be you. This earthly life is a school from which we learn from and who we are is our key to our journey. The abilities we have at birth are our tools for success. Slip through the cracks and find that magic in you.... I hope you enjoy my story.

Contents

This is a true story. All names and places have been changed to protect the privacy of all. Every person's journey is their own. Everyone will experience their own abilities in their own way.

The Word "God" in this book does not represent "One God" view. It represents a Universal Consciousness

I dedicate this book to my family who's love,
encouragement and patients made this book possible.
-namaste-

*"The Essential Lesson I've
Learned in life is to
Just be yourself.
Treasure the Magnificent
Being that you are."*
                    -Wayne Dyer

Through the Cracks

The Beginning

July 10, 1994, I married into a family that for many years made me feel like I was an outsider. I could never find the bonds one would in a family. I was from what most people in this day would call from across the tracks. I was born to a single mother who had no motherly or domestic skills. She had many children by different men most of which were taken away and placed in foster care due to abuse and neglect and I was one of them. Her favorite social skill when she wasn't visiting the truck stops meeting men, was the bar down the street where she would spend most of her time. She would lock me and my sisters in a closet as she went out for the night. Some would think that a childhood like that would be traumatizing to a child. To me as a child it opened me up to who I was to become. To some of my other siblings it only created emotional scars and to one sister lifelong physical and mental issues. During these years, the years that are about development and nurturing. I was neglected and never had the loving nurturing that a young child would receive from a mother therefore I was never taught how to form bonds with others and I carried that through my adult years.

I, through my childhood, had many experiences that became a normal part of me. Inside my closet, I could astral travel with ease so to escape the darkness of the small room. The more I spent in the closet and in this world of no structure the more my gifts would develop because there was no one to teach me differently. My friends were the spirits that came to visit or that had residence in the house I lived in. These gifts made me different in a way that most people could not accept and my new family was not an exception. I was the woman who broke all the rules to what they believed and everything that they had brought their family up to be, I defied it all.

I came with what they called baggage from another family, 3 children of my own and if that wasn't enough I was 9 years older than my new husband. This was not all bonding material for this family.

When my husband met, me he saw the magic I held within me, he saw what everyone was so afraid of in their conventional life. I was not conventional in any way. All my experiences made me unique and it all came natural to me. I could tap into the spirit world; I could read other people with just a touch or the feeling of their energy. My spiritual beliefs and values held roots in Witchcraft that cast fear and doubt within the family structure. Through my husband's childhood his beliefs left him with many questions in life, so he took it upon himself to search for those answers among my world. While doing so he found his place and vowed to help me find my ground in a world that only looked at me as different and dark. Together we embraced my spirituality and he promised to learn all he could.

It was not long before he too adapted my spirituality and we swore to raise any of the children we may have with the same values. This created an even bigger wedge in the family for me. This was the first time in my life that I was out of the spiritual closet and I had no idea how to blend it all within this family. I had not had anyone in my life that ever understood who I was or what gifts I had. No one had ever taken the time to see me for the person I was without labels, without judgement. My husband did, but his family was a different story.

Holidays and family gatherings were hard. I could feel the uncomfortable energy and judgement that filled the room. I would sit among them as they laughed and talked and shared their bonds. At times, I felt like the woman in the corner that no one spoke to. Gift giving at Christmas time was elaborate for all. For me it was filled with tote bags and candles that came free with a purchase of someone else's gift because they "didn't know what to get me" nor did they care to find out. To them I held something dark with in me and to ignore that somehow made that easier for them. I was happy with that though, growing up in foster care did not present anything more than that either. I was just as happy to find my place among the spirits that passed through like I would as a child. I would also tap into the energy of the holiday and listen to the chaotic thoughts of the others. No one knew that I could hear their thoughts it was a secret that I found was better kept to myself and believe me I wasn't the only one that had negative thoughts brewing in someone's mind. They all gave me a clear understanding of what it is to love and hate at the same time.

Hearing thoughts and reading energy by just a mere touch sometimes had to be kept a secret. This was who I was all my life. I did not know how to change it and making that known would cause more apprehension with others. They already thought I was the "Evil one" and that I had some underhanded agenda. At times, it was hard, I would hear the thoughts when my back was turned or not looking at the person and I would respond. When that happened, I had to back track and cover my tracks. Other times I would hear the thought so loud that I would be startled at the sound. I would jump or react in some way that looked ridiculous and had to explain why I had that reaction. Then there would be times when it was just a whisper and I would respond with" Did you say something?" or "what did you say?" everyone in the room at that moment would respond, "I didn't say anything." Only once did someone say to me, "how did you know what I was thinking I have not asked the question yet?" when I answered her question while my back was turned. For many years, I had a hard time distinguishing thoughts to words, so I had to pay close attention.

These energies and experiences would drain me so I learned how to shield myself so the energy didn't collapse me. Going to a mall or anywhere that there was chaotic energy hurt me like kryptonite did to superman. Shielding became a constant. (*{see appendix}* and In time I learned how to shut it off. Up until I learned how to shut it off relationships were hard and crowds were avoided.

Most people today when they experience emotional pain or another person violates their trust that causes personal trust issues, they build up walls to protect themselves, don't let others in. Me? I open all my senses so I can see, so I can feel. Let it take its course. Emotions can cause blocks that would hinder my gifts and clog my chakra. (*see appendix*) This was not an easy task and required me to see and feel all that hurt me. I had to learn to deal with life in ways that were not common for others.

The gifts I hold would allow me to see way beyond the spectrum that most people could. Many people wished they had those gifts. They wanted to be me. The shows and movies they would see on television where the medium or psychic would be trusted and idolized, looked up to and were making a living helping people was just not my world. To be who I am is living and seeing the world in a different way even with my own family. People live on physical proof and just to know something doesn't make life easy. It is explaining how you know and then the doubts and the this and that's that the other person has. The "you don't know that for sure." Comments. Made it very tough. Being me is just not as glamourous as people think. Having the gift of seeing and knowing sometimes just seemed worthless. People just do not accept the explanation of "I just know", or" I can see it." My only recourse was to fabricate a story that would give me the verification I needed for people to listen and accept what I was seeing and knowing as fact so that their life would be on the right path or to protect people I loved. Sometimes it was just to heal a broken heart with a message from a loved one who has passed. That to became hard. I lived a life that everyone wanted but nobody knew what it entailed. When people thought that you might have some psychic abilities they would want immediate proof. "Well tell me the winning numbers to the lottery." They would say. The lottery is all about probability. When something happens that surprises, me I hear, "your psychic you should have known that was going to happen" what they do not know is that all psychics are not wired for sound 24/7 they would be burnt out, and sometimes we doubt our own abilities or just do not want to see it because it is too close to our own hearts. We are human after all.

Then there is the side of being human and people close to you do not accept that your knowing is a benefit for them; For instance, my son who is a fantastic athlete. He has played football through elementary and high school, four-year letterman, starting fullback/linebacker. Won many of awards academically and athletically. Going to college on an athletic scholarship with a Major in Pre-Med. For years, I would say thing to him what coaches would say or do before they did them, what they thought of him what was going through their minds about what he did on that field that day. He would constantly ask me how I knew. Well knowing the "I just know" answer did not work; I would say I talked to this person or that person. Although it was more than that, I had actually seen them and read them either by a touch or other abilities I had. It would set his mind at ease and come the next time he was to see the coach he would find I was correct and that would be the end of it. When I would tell him how good he was he would say to me "mom, you are my mother you have to say that." He knew better, he knew that I say how I see it, sugar coating is not something I subscribe to. For him to listen I had to fabricate a story that he would understand so not to steer him away from his goals. I saw his future before he was born and I was going to do whatever I could to get him to where he was to be. With College Coaches, I would say they emailed me which was possible because they had my email address on the applications. Then he would start saying "show me", so I said I talked to them. In reality it was a vision. When my son went to football camp, I told him he would win Gridiron Elite the highest award they give. He just said, "Mom, I doubt it." At the end of the week we went and picked him up and at the award ceremony he was the recipient of Gridiron Elite award and 2 other awards on top of that. He did this 2 years in a row. In the end, I was right and it not only kept the positive flow of positive energy moving forward each time it kept him moving forward and not be tripped up by insecurity of not knowing. The information was not always "hey dude you did a great job, your awesome" It was about "straighten up, you know you did not do it right, your better than that.". He just did not have to wait and waste time worrying about it all the time. This was all his dream and his destiny my gifts just helped get him there and kept him going in a straight line at times when he would get off balanced.

Millersville University was his chosen goal and obstacles fell in his way. I knew he would achieve his goal, he just needed to see it and keep moving forward. Some of the obstacles were people who just kept throwing road blocks his way. My encouragement at sometimes seemed hard but I saw this for him, I had this knowing, he just had to believe it Daniel knew that it was not going to be easy and at times was tiring just having to jump over those road blocks. Every day I would say two things to him "One negative thought can be the difference of winning and losing" a quote I read on Facebook that resonated with me and what I was trying to instill in my son and "Daniel, we are not from here, make them see. the right people will look. When he missed National Signing day, Daniel was heartbroken but I knew it was not over yet. I picked Daniel up, and told him in no uncertain terms that I had no doubt, I saw him there this was not over.

He got offers from other schools, many, and some of those offers were extremely generous. He got over night invites to get pampered by some schools in hopes he would choose their school. One particular school said to him "Daniel, why not be a big fish in a small pond." And Daniels reply to that amazed me and I knew I had finally got the message through to him. "Coach, with all respect, a big fish cannot grow in a small pond, It can only grow as big as the pond it is in, I want to grow. Thank you for the offer."

After all the Obstacles and road blocks, Daniel got his opportunity he was dreaming of and is on the Roster playing football at Millersville University. He is now a small fish in a big pond growing every day.

Last night I saw his name and number on the Jersey of a NFL player of Daniel favorite team. I sent it to Daniel. On to next Dream.

Locked Away, Never Alone

I was taken away from my mother and separated from my siblings at a young age due to my mother's abuse, neglect, and inability to care for me and my siblings.

It was in the 1960" s, I was almost 4 years old and life with my mother did not seem to affect me much. I came into this world not as an infant but with some type of knowing and ability to survive. I was not like other kids, when I fell and scraped my knee, I did not cry and run to mommy to kiss it and make it feel better. I got up brushed it off, shrug my shoulders and moved on.

I did not have much for toys, I am sure I had some but do not remember any, so I used my imagination and created my own toys.

Many people that came around thought I was strange. I

was too smart for my age and would just watch them like I was waiting for them to do something, it made them feel uncomfortable.

I did not trust with ease and was fully aware that there were good people and bad people. At times, I would carefully touch people, by doing so I would know if I did not like them. If I did not I would gather up my siblings and hide in a safe place I knew all too well. The Closet. My mother and the strangers would laugh at me thinking I was just a strange little girl that was spooked by strangers, but I was not fearful of much.

For as long as I could remember my mother locking us in the closet when she left to go to the bar and often forget about us when she got home because she was drunk and would pass out. My other siblings were afraid but I was not, to me the Closet was like a magical room and a safe place. When I wanted to see, what was happening outside of the closet I would close my eyes and be still. I would see myself outside my body and I would rise up outside of the closet and watch and listen to what was happening and go back and tell my sisters. I had the ability to astral travel, I called it my super power. I did not know what it was that I was doing till later on in my life. I was astral traveling.

Astral traveling is easier for a young child, especially a child before the age of 5. A child does not fully ground into earthly body until the age of 5 when upon entering school they are taught to use reasoning and logic and they start using the left side of the brain and are mainstreamed into other ways of thinking. They are guided and taught earthly human values. They start to forget who they are and how they became human. Their vibrations start to slow down. The natural abilities they were born with start to fade.

I was not mainstreamed; my mother was not the domestic motherly type. She had a disturbed childhood being brought up by family members since she was 13 years old in a life full of abuse and alcohol. In her adult life she had other children taken away by the children and youth service from neglect and abuse. So, raising children was not a skill my mother had and honestly, we were just a burden. I often wonder how I managed to survive at such a young age. My siblings were older than me but I was the older soul, I took care of them.

I was almost four when I was taken away from my mother. I remembered that day like it was yesterday. Although my mother had no domestic skills I still felt comfortable and safe there it was the one place I knew. I had never been beyond that house and what made it worse was I was separated from my siblings and I needed them and they needed me. It was 30 years before I was able to see one of them again and the trauma left her with handicaps but still in a glimpse of a moment she remembered our closet. My other sibling I never saw again or my mother.

Good-Bye Great Grandpa

After many foster homes that did not work out and being abandoned at a hospital by a foster family, finally, at the age of 5, I was placed in a foster home where they hoped I would find some roots, a home that was to be permanent. Deep down so did I. The family was nice, warm and loving. I felt happy and fit right in.

They had 2 boys of their own that instantly became my little brothers. I learned how to be a little girl.

We lived on a Audubon in Greenwich Connecticut, My foster father worked there so we lived in a house right on the Audubon. I loved it there. I didn't feel like a number or an orphan, I felt like a sister, a daughter and most of all a family.

The house in Greenwich was old and I had a little room upstairs all to myself and it was there that I met Sarah. Sarah was a little girl spirit that would come and visit me, I could see and talk to her, she was my secret friend. I did not want to tell anyone because I did not want this family to leave me like the others.

It was here I discovered my abilities to communicate with the Afterlife and to be able to see and hear them. That was my secret. I could not understand why other people could not do what seemed so natural for me. At the young age of five years old I had this knowing that there was more Beyond this human experience.

It was four years before I was taken from them and placed in another home but those years I had many more experiences with the afterlife and what we call the spirit world.

At age six my experiences broadened. My foster grandparents lived on this beautiful estate in Greenwich where my grandfather was a caretaker. The main house was huge with many windows, It would take grandfather days to wash the outside of all the windows. The house had a ghost I would see in the windows at times standing looking out across the estate. Sometimes it was a woman in what looked like a long dress others times it was a man in a dress suit. I loved it there. The care takers house in which my grandparents lived was a beautiful stone house.

The House had many rooms and a long hallway. The kitchen was like that of a restaurant kitchen with 2 kinds of stoves. The grounds had a little pond where I used to skate in the winter and rows of cherry trees where I and my brothers would spend hours picking delicious cherries.

There was also this little stone one room house covered in ivy and moss set across from the garden that I believed they used to put gardening tools, but Uncle Bob and my foster father thought it was the perfect spot to put in a train set complete with scenery and it took up half of the room. I used to sit at the end of one side of the track and put my chin right at the end of the table so the train would come right at me and then swiftly take the corner. I could do that for hours at a time.

Sometimes late at night I could hear the whistle of the

locomotive and see the lights as the train passed the tiny window when everyone was sound asleep.

That Estate had many spirits that kept me company through the years. My great grandfather knew of my abilities and knew that I had the abilities to see hear and speak to spirits. I felt comforted by that.

He would tell me how special I was and not to forget it because my special abilities would help me see the world in true light.

Great-Grandpa would play the piano with me and take walks in the garden. Saturday mornings were my favorite times, he would come out of his room early to watch Saturday morning cartoons with me.

He loved Road runner, Foghorn leghorn and good ole bugs bunny and to this day I can still hear him laughing, he would laugh so hard that when the morning of cartoons was done he would grab his cane and walk to his room laughing and mumbling all the way to take a nap. He would sleep for an hour or so as I waited patiently for him to awaken then we would have lunch and on summer days spend time in the garden tending to the flowers as I told him about my stories with my friends.

Great-grandpa was in his late eighties and at times talked about journeying. into the next lifetime. He used to talk about meeting his friends, his wife and angels on the other side. I used to hear him talking to people in his room telling them he would be there soon, he was ready.

One afternoon great grandpa did not get up from his nap, as I entered his room to wake him, I saw his physical body lying in bed but his spirit self was outside his body, he smiled and waved to me as I stood at the end of his bed. "remember you are special, keep your eyes open, your ears listening and you heart true." he whispered as he vanished. His body still laying peaceful in his bed. I knew then I had just witnessed my great-grandfather transition beyond his human body.

It did not take long before my grandmother came in and realize that Great-grandpa had passed. She rushed me out of the room and quickly called the Doctor and ambulance.

I sat on the couch in the living room wondering where he went and why hadn't anyone else experienced this transition. Why didn't he seem sad or afraid? He was happy and peaceful as I saw him lift from his earthly body.

I as a young child, was not afraid either and I did not feel sad. It was like he was going home or on vacation. At his funeral, everyone was crying and telling stories of past times. The Pastor read verses of him being with God and how when we die we will see him again. It was at that moment things changed, I interrupted with "No he isn't with God, he is right there" as I point beside the coffin, and he is with Great-grandma see him?" I said. I could hear the gasps and then the silence. I was then taken by the hand and put into the car to be dealt with later. I watched out the window as I saw Great-grandpa go to everyone and then he went on his journey and complete his transition into the spirit world. Some call this Death.

As a child, we are told that someday we all will die never to see our loved ones again, that life had a beginning and an ending and we never know when our life will be over. It was all so infinite and so sad. I knew differently. My great grandfather didn't just end. I saw him lift out of his body and wave to me as he spoke my name. He was not sad then and he was not sad as he made his rounds at his funeral.

That was my great-grandfather who was my friend and he appeared to be so full of life and whom spoke to me many times after that. So, what was death?

"You are not a drop in the ocean
You are the entire ocean in a drop"
                                        -Rumi-

The Gift of Spirit

Most people today are afraid of spirits because they represent death. Death is one of the most feared aspects of life. Seeing and communicating with spirits became another constant in my life. I grew up with that ability as natural to me as the air we breathe. I was born with all these natural abilities. I was never mainstreamed to believe or be anything other than who I am. I was just a number in the foster care system moving from home to home with no roots and no one to recognize the gifts that I had and was born with. I moved from foster home to foster home not being able to establish roots I was just case number 1-9d 5689 or something like that. When I would show what, they would view as abnormal behavior they would make a phone call and off to another foster home I would go. It happened so much I would be used to it and when I saw the State worker unexpectedly, I would go and pack my toys, say good bye to my spirit friends and go right to the car.

One foster home in Stanford Ct, The Johnsons woke up in the middle of the night and heard me talking to my spirit friends and the next day they brought me to the hospital called the state and left me there. The report was that I was showing very disturbing behavior and they could no longer have me among their other children they felt I was a danger. From that point on I was labeled as disturbed. Which made it harder for me to find that forever home.

As I got older my gifts continued and progressed. When I was in my early teens I was placed in a home in Tolland Connecticut and they feared me so much that they would lock me in my room when I was not in school. The monthly check for an emotionally disturbed child was much more than the regular "Normal" children so keeping me there was a big benefit and to them well worth it.

I was locked in my room upstairs from the outside, when it was time to eat they would knock and open the door for me to get my food and eat. They fed me well and at times when the Foster mother was feeling good, maybe from the wine she drank daily she would allow me downstairs at the dinner table and at times to socialize. The house was so dirty and cluttered I did not mind staying in my room. There were other foster children in the home as well but they got special treatment. One girls name was Debbie; she was a bit on the rebellious side and would constantly sneak out and get herself in trouble. She liked me. Debbie knew of my gifts and was very intrigued and her being older with more privileges she could bring me some what they called then occult tools. Debbie loved the tarot cards and she taught me all the identity of the cards then she would play this memory game with them with me to test my abilities. She would place the cards on my forehead and I would tell her what the card was without looking at the card. This excited Debbie and soon she was teaching me how to read the tarot cards and I was showing her more of who I was.

One night Debbie climbed out the window and went out

with her usual friends and got arrested. She was with the wrong crowd they were drinking and smoking marijuana. Debbie did not go to jail because she was just the innocent tag along but she did get taken away and I never saw her again after that. Debbie did do me one favor though, she told the state what was happening to me and by surprise one day the state came for a visit. First they came to the school and asked me questions and then they came to the house. Just the condition of the house was warrant enough, but they also found the Foster Mother drunk during the day as well.

Debbie was the first person to recognize my abilities and would always tell me I had the "Gift of Spirit" and that I was special in ways most people could never understand and she hoped I would be free one day to be who I am.

"God is always within, Feel God working in your heart
Through your heart and as your heart."
-Roxana Jones-

The Devil Within

Society has labels that they use to describe things they do not understand. Many are created by their own religious beliefs and fear. Many were taught that the gifts that I held were works of the devil. Since I had no religious upbringing that would cleanse my soul I was described as influenced by the devil.

By the Time I was placed in the home of The Smith Family I was in my teens and had already had my own view of Religion, the afterlife and my gifts, after all I had direct communication with the afterlife so I knew what life and death was about. I never feared or questions my abilities it was others that did.

The Smiths, knew me when I was younger but never knew of who I was, but knew all I had been through. As a Christian family, they felt that their love and religious structure would shape me into a fine young lady and all the torment I had been through in my life would be healed and I would be Saved. Saved being the key word. Their intentions were good. The Smiths were in no way bad people they were warm and loving and just wanted the best for me, but that meant much work. They had to strip me of all of what they thought was bad influences or inappropriate for a young teenager. That meant cloths, no more fashionable jeans or low cut shirts, tee-shirts were for boys and young ladies wore blouses. High heels were for hussies, skirts and dresses below the knee and only one button was allowed unbuttoned on blouse or you were being tempting to men or boys. Make-up Never. My records were discarded and replaced with gospel. Television was limited and dating was a big No, any school dances were accompanied by one of their older sons. I entered my new high school looking like a scared puritan girl from some religious school all dressed in brown and white. Brown and white the main color of my wardrobe. That was the worst thing I ever experienced, it took away my identity. I felt like I had a mask on that was hiding who I was. Going to high school wearing buster brown shoes? Where were my converse, my perfectly fitted bell bottom jeans, my tightly fitted v-cut shirt that conformed to my figure like a glove and my black leather fringe jacket that I loved like it was my best friend, my moccasins and high black boots? My pocket book and make-up case. They took them all. I wanted to scream, and hide.

That day when I got home from school I went to my room and cried. I stayed in my room all night and never came out for dinner. The next few days I pretended to be sick and stayed home from school dreading having to go back looking like I did the first day. The Smiths soon thought I was having adjustment problems and agreed for me to have a tutor come to the house and edge me back into mainstream school. During that time, when I was helping with dinner I had to go to the basement and get some vegetables for dinner. Mrs. Smith always had shelves in the basement loaded with overstock of canned goods. In the corner, next to the shelves were a stack of boxes that had my name on them. My heart raced with excitement. Was that my stuff? I got called back upstairs so I could not open the boxes to see what was in them but I had hope that some of the things I loved dearly were in those boxes.

After dinner when everyone went to bed I laid awake waiting for everyone to go to sleep so I could sneak down in the basement and see what was in those boxes. You would think those boxes held hidden treasures or great amounts of gold. I opened the boxes and there was all my stuff. My make-up, I could smell the aroma of my perfume emerging from the box. There all folded up were my jeans and my cloths, there was all of me in a box. For the first time in months I felt connected again. I grabbed a few things and my make-up and brought them upstairs and hid them in my drawer up in my room and I would wear one of my shirts under my clothing just to have a part of me.

For about 6months being at the Smiths I had no contact with any spirits and my other abilities seemed to be off balance. I accredited that to the fact that I was off balance because of the whole change this family was inflicting on me. For all my life, I had been the same person, no one noticed me unless I was doing something that they felt was disturbed then they without any further understanding sent me packing. I do believe that the Smiths did want to give me a better life with stability and structure, it was great for their children why not me?

One day I was downstairs in the basement helping with household chores like laundry which I helped to do so that I could wash and dry some of my hidden cloths. I was back in school so I wear them under my outfits or sneak into my bag and change into when no one was looking before school.

As I was downstairs I started to feel and see a presence of a teenage girl. Where this might make some people fearful, it made me happy. I can imagine how that might sound to some of you that are reading this, all the things going through your head describing the kind of person I was and still am today. "This teenage girl did not feel complete again until she saw spirits again, and she did not fear them she was happy!" In most Religious upbringing that would make me some sort of evil.

In the 1970's and still today many religious belief systems define the ability to talk to the dead as a demonic practice. This family was no different. It did not take them much longer to discover the abilities that I had and after what seemed like a lifetime of being lost I had found me again and was not afraid to show it. The difference with this family than any other was they were determined to find the root of who I was. They did not call the state and throw me out or leave me in some hospital, they were determined to fix me as they thought and it did come from a place of love.

The Smiths had met me when I was with another foster family and was taken away from them because of a murder of an 18month old child that had happened in that family. The state would not allow them to take me at that time because they thought it would be better for me to be placed out of the area. I had been in 3 other homes before they allowed the Smiths to take me. I was best friends with their oldest daughter and they wanted to give me the best that they could offer.

They set me up with Doctors and Psychologists, they had EEGs done on me in fear that there was a medical reason I was like I was. To no avail did they find any medical reason I had the abilities I have.

The Smiths were a big part of the born again Christian movement and since there was no medical reason for what they called my inflictions they took me to their church where they thought for sure they would be able to save me. They had me go to weekly church meetings and counseling with the Reverend at The First Assembly of God. It was their findings that told them that I was among the Devil realm and needed to be cleansed of his influence therefor I needed to be baptized, they thought if I was baptized it would rid me of my abilities and I would be saved and able to be a "normal" teenager.

It was not too soon after that, I picked up and left. I had lived with them for a few years by then and I got a good sense of family. The Smiths were a very close family. Dinner was served at the same time and everyone sat at the table together, the girls baked on weekends. Homework was done and checked every night. The whole family dynamics was run with a strict hand. They loved me but they did not understand who I was. They could not see beyond their own Religious structure. When I left I never saw them again? I often wonder if they ever wondered what happened to me.

Although this family was deeply rooted with in their Religious beliefs they never stepped out of the circle of love. They did not understand my gifts or how they were apart of who I was but never did they judge me or turn their back on me. They did what only they knew how to do.

Organized Religion had in that time closed doors for people like me. There is only one explanation that organized religion gave to understand who I am. I believe in my heart that The Smiths knew that but they also knew I was the exception to their rule. They did not know how a touch of my hand could tell me their inner soul, or how I could see the future that they were taught only the Divine could see or how I could talk to people who had passed like they were right there in the room with me. What they did know is I was not evil or dangerous and I did not have the devil within me. So, when I left, they let me go and they did so the only way they knew. With Love.

"Remind yourself that you cannot fail
At being yourself"

-Wayne Dyer-

Daddy's Girl

The road back to the only family I had where I felt part of, was a short and easy one because after leaving Tolland I was taken back to the town that they had taken me from years before. The place I was happy, where for a mere time I had a mother, a father, and 2 brothers and a baby sister. My neighborhood, my bus stop, my house, the tree where my foster dad built my tree house and my initials were deeply carved into, just a mile away.

I walked the roads remembering all the memories, the sounds, the smells. It had been almost 5 years since I lived there and walked these roads. I was not allowed to while living with the Smiths because they thought it would be to traumatizing for me. Now I was eager. I had not had any contact with them all this time. As I walked I remembered where my dad and I shot our first squirrel, I could still smell the smell of the gun and hear the shot in my ear. I stopped and looked over the cliff and remembered when I drove my mini bike for the first time over the edge of the cliff, my brothers ran over and helped me back up the hill with the mini bike first checking to see if I was ok then the mini bike hoping I had not damaged it and like little boys do when their sister almost totaled their favorite toy, they cussed all the way up that embankment "stupid sister" "Girls should stick with dolls mini bikes are for boys,"

As I approached the house I could almost hear the sound of my dad in the garage restoring his 1952 Chevy Belair. He had two that I could remember, one was a powder blue and the other one, my favorite was Red and White. He was a mechanic by trade and loved to restore old cars, ride his motorcycle and play his banjo and ukulele. I sat on the stone wall of this now vacant house remembering it all like it was a movie on a screen. I thought about the last days there. With my family, the ones who wanted to adopt me. I was almost nine years old when the car pulled up and loaded all my belonging in the trunk and took me away. It seemed all too familiar. The tears ran down my face as the words" I am sorry" were repeating in my head. This was supposed to be my family, my forever home, but tragedy struck and I was a witness to it and the home had to be closed. I remember the events that led up to that day like it was yesterday.

After moving from the Audubon in Greenwich, Ct to the house in Ridgefield, Ct my foster parents whom we will call Elizabeth and Jerry Peterson for the sake of this book. Decided that they would open their home up to another foster child, this time this one would be an infant right from the hospital. She was a beautiful little girl that took to my heart the moment she came home to us. We nicknamed her Korky, I do not remember why we called her that I think it was because of her long ethnic birth name. We never used her birth name we just called her Korky.

During the next few months Jerry and Elizabeth split up due to an extra marital affair but we still stayed with Elizabeth and there was no talk of us having to be taken out of the home at that point. Jerry moved out and like any family that had a marital breakup we would have our weekends with Jerry. They were very good at keeping adult problems with adults so we never knew what was going on or saw their anger toward each other. Although I knew. I could feel the energy and the hurt and I could see what had happened. Temptation if not resisted is a turning point in any relationship. Elizabeth was a good and loving mother, still today I can feel her soft touch of her hands. For me it was so hard to see and feel her pain. She was the only real mother I had and I loved her. I loved her nurturing energy it made me feel loved and a part of a family. I did not like this feeling of pain and sadness I felt from her now. This is where I learned what sadness and heartache felt like. Most of the emotions I felt as a child I learned from other people, I could feel their pain and heartache, their fear and of course their joy.

As time went on Elizabeth started dating other men. Elizabeth would soon find a man that she would form a relationship with named Cliff, he seemed very nice. He would take us places and spend time with us and buy us ice cream. When Elizabeth was working some nights, he would be our babysitter when our regular babysitter Valerie was not available. Cliff would join us for dinner most nights and as time went on I started to feel uneasy around him. His energy made me feel uncomfortable at times sick to my stomach. When he would play with korky I would get this immediate urge to take her from him and run. When I told Elizabeth about that feeling she said that it was just because I felt like a little mother to korky and it was only natural that I would feel so protective. I watched him constantly and just could not shake that feeling. Cliff would complain always saying that we would give the baby to much attention and that we spoiled her way too much, so when he would babysit at times he would just close the door and let her scream in her crib till she went to sleep, sometimes for hours. Cliff seemed angry when anyone would show their attention to her. When I think about it now I wonder if it was because of her ethnic background, Cliff seemed to have race issues and when no one was listening he had remarks about Korky being from ethnic mix race parents.

One night Elizabeth had to go out, she did home parties for extra money, our other babysitter was busy that night so Cliff offered to babysit. Something inside of me felt like this was not a good idea, Cliff seemed off, like he was angry at the world. At dinner that night he started an argument with Elizabeth. Korky did not like to hear loud yelling, it scared her, so she cried. Elizabeth tended to her and soothed her. Cliff was so angry because he thought he was being ignored so he got up threw his napkin and fork on the table and with anger pointed at Korky and yelled "That baby is spoiled rotten and more important than me!!" he exited to the living room. Elizabeth calmed down the baby and reassured me and my brothers it would be alright. Elizabeth did manage to calm Cliff down and soon the situation seems to have been solved and they were smiling all looked well.

The time came for Elizabeth to leave for her home party. It had been my turn to clear the table and do the dishes, me and my brothers would take turns doing them. Elizabeth kissed us all good bye told us to be good. My brothers were still at the dining room table finishing dinner and korky in her high chair as I cleared the table. As I was in the kitchen Cliff came and took Korky out of her high chair and to my surprise started playing with her, I heard her giggling and then I heard Cliff say "WeeeeeWeeeee". I hurried up with dishes and then went to look at all the fun as I was thinking;" Momma must have really said something really good to make him like korky because he never played with her". I go into the hallway and there is Cliff throwing Korky in the air, "weee"... he said I gasped as he threw her higher and higher, my stomach was feeling funny and I began to have that feeling again. Then he threw her up one last time and stepped away. He did not catch her; he didn't even try he let her fall to the ground. She screamed an awful scream, he picked her up and put her in her bed screaming. I tried to go to her, he yelled at me and told us all to go to bed. My brothers slept in bunkbeds in the room with Korky and her crib. My brothers went to their beds and I went to my room. I heard him yell at my brother to roll over and face the wall. I was afraid, I knew something bad was happening, I could not stay in my room so I went to sneak and help Korky. I watched from outside the room in the hallway and saw Cliff try and get the baby to stand, she couldn't, he shook her and told her to stop crying, she just screamed more, just then I watched this man slam korky head in the wall, not once but twice I gasped, Cliff turned and saw me frozen with tears in my eyes "Didn't I tell you to go to bed?" he yelled as he shut the door.

Korky died 2 weeks later, she was in a coma and paralyzed from the neck down and I was the only witness. Korky was 18months old.

I sat on the stone wall remembering those horrible times with tears streaming down my face when I hear a familiar voice say, "I knew you would one day find your way home." I turned around and tears of sadness turned to tears of joy "Daddy!" I said. It had been years but my daddy, the only one I ever had. Jerry Peterson still looked the same just like I remembered and he knew me.

Jerry had remarried, He married the woman across the street, Elizabeth's best friend Sherri. Daddy was excited to see me and asked me to come stay with them and continue school. My dad worked as a mechanic and was in the process of building an established business in another state, a state in which he had bought a house. Sherri did not want to up root her life or sell her home so my dad would travel back every two weeks.

My dad had contacted the State and told them that I would be staying with him and asked them to ask the Smith to let him come and get my stuff. When he came back with the boxes in the basement I was so excited I could not wait to have my Tarot cards again. Sherri and I spent much time together while dad was away. I was not much of a talker and kept to myself on most occasions. I spent hours with my tarot cards connecting with them and re-learning what they meant. I spent much time remembering all that Debbie had taught me a short while ago.

Sherri always reminded me of a young Sophia Loren, she had that beauty and grace, she made jeans and a flannel shirt look fashionable. I love her style and independence.

She was an artist and spent much time painting outside on the patio or in what I called it the All-season room because it was surrounded by large windows and had no heat in the winter.

When Sherri painted, I could see a shadow of herself like her soul would expand and be the artist, it was like watching a double shadow image of her painting at the Easel. She was lost in her art and nothing could interrupt that moment in time for her and I was amazed. At times when I knew she was discovering the beauty in her art I would see what I know today as her aura, her emotions in color around her and if your sensitive like me you could feel the energy explode if you were in the room or around her. She was a natural artist and I loved the gifts she opened inside of me. Most people are sheltered with their energy they keep it hidden or close to them and I never had the experience to see and feel the aura and the energy like that but when Sherri was alone she opened like a morning glory in the morning sun.

This experience helped me with my other gifts. With the tarot, it brought certain images out of the cards and I no longer needed to study the book that came with the cards, the meanings became my own.

The summer went quick and Sherri was getting tired of living separate from her husband so we packed up and moved to Dads house in New York. My dad had given me as a gift one of those beaded pocketbooks with the draw string so I carried my cards with me, I never wanted to be separated from them again.

The house was an old farm house in a small country town.

It was nothing like Sherri's quaint cabin style home set in a wooded area. This was a big white farm house on a main route with flat open land that stretched for miles. What it did have was spirits.

I do not know why no one else but me and the cat and dog knew there were other occupants in the house, but I felt it the moment I stepped foot on the property.

Most people view spirits as dark and evil but to this day I have never encountered such a spirit. mischievous and playful maybe but never dark and evil. I was not really good at seeing spirits yet at this point or at least I did not think so. But, I could feel and hear. One would think that since I could see energy and intense aura then I would be able to easily see spirits at that time. This was not true for me. When I saw the energies from Sherri it was more of an uncontrolled energy if you do not know you are doing it. Sherri was in her free unabridged moment and completely open and she did not know anyone was watching and no one was aware of my special abilities yet. A spirit on the other hand has the control and knowing.

I was elated by this and was not in any way uncomfortable or fearful. The spirits gave me someone to talk to. Sherri had two kids of her own but we were not close, we used to be as young children before I was taken away, but as a young teenager I was the threat because to them I was daddy's girl. He was all I had and I held tight to him. Sherri's children got whatever they wanted and that was ok with me I just wanted my stuff and occasionally stuff that I needed like cloths I outgrew or socks and under garments and my dad. I had a special bond with my dad that to me was real like we were blood somehow.

I did share a room with Layla, Sherri's daughter who was the youngest of us all and she posed me more problems than the spirits did. Layla was always snooping in my stuff. I always wrote journals and when I was done writing them I would put them in a plastic sealed bag and bury them Layla found this out by reading my journals she also discovered through my journals that I spoke to spirits. At first Sherri just shrugged it off as me using my imagination and telling stories for attention so at times I would have to endure the teasing of Layla and her little snoopy friends. They would try and play tricks on me, jump out at me, and whatever they could to try and scare me. I just shook my head and brushed it off.

One day when I came home from school I found Sherri in my room and my cards on my bed and my journal in her hand, my heart fell to the floor all my secrets in her hand and by her face and her energy it was not happy time. My life the past year was in that book, my study of the cards and the things I saw and did with my gifts all of it. "This is evil" she said "do you know what this is? This is devils work; how dare you have this around my children in my house, I knew there was something not right with you, I keep telling your father that, you are not that daddy's little girl he once knew, you wait, just wait till your father comes home" I stayed in my room feeling lost and afraid tears ran down my face for the first time in what seemed like a lifetime. I heard Sherri down stairs on the phone she had called Mr. Henry my case worker and told him he would have to find a new home for me because it was not working out, she feels I have deep rooted problems that could danger her 2 children. My heart sank, she had gotten me all wrong, I was not a danger to her children and I surely was not evil. I had gifts, gifts that through the years I have developed with my own life experiences. Gifts I was born with.

Sherri hung up the phone and called her children to the kitchen. She showed them my journal and my tarot card and asked them if they knew about these things? If I had done something to them or influenced them in any way? The woman who never went to church or even showed any religious affiliation, we never even said prayers at dinner time was now acting like she had seen the devil herself and he was about to take over the world and her house was home base.

I sat on my bed holding back the tears. I was good at that had much practice in my younger years, I feel the emotion inside but hold back the emotion on the outside. I started thinking, was I that different? Is there something wrong with me? I had had seizures when I was a young child and EEG's of my brain, but that proved to be normal and I grew out of the seizures. I felt fine. I do not have bad thoughts or angry feelings I just keep to myself. I have friends even a boyfriend so I am not socially disconnected. I guess you can say I just do not like the feeling of some people's energy and some of the thoughts that go through their head so I prefer to stay away.

I sat on the edge of my bed for what seemed like hours wondering what I will do next. Where I will go I was too old to just leave at a hospital and I was not going to go to another foster home.

I heard daddy's truck pull in the driveway and the door shut. I cover my ears with my hands and closed my eyes I couldn't bare to hear the disappointment and the rejection in his voice. It seemed like hours when I felt the heat and presence of someone standing in front of me. I took the hands off my ears opened my eyes and look up and my daddy was standing in front of me. In his hands were my journal and my tarot cards and an old metal lock box. He looked down at me and said to me Are these yours? I am sorry that Sherri invaded your privacy, here is a box to lock them in so this will not happen again," I was surprised that he was not mad at me. He sat down next to me on my bed and gave me his fatherly hug and told me to never mind Sherri she just does not understand teenagers.

My dad was ok and nothing changed with us but it did with me and Sherri and her two children. I was the evil step child and Sherri was upset that my dad didn't just throw me out.

As the tension built between us and the harsh treatment Sherri and her kids gave me I made plans to leave.

I had an older boyfriend still back home and I made plans to go and visit, so I told my dad. He helped me book an Amtrak ticket and took me to the station. I remember the look in his eyes when he handed me my pillow, he knew I was not coming back. "I love you and you will always be daddy's girl he said as the train door shut.

When I was 15years of age, after going through many home placements I decides to take the matters into my own hands and emancipate myself from the system and make it on my own. They allowed that without even a court hearing or discussion on the issue. So, I did just that.

To me being in the care of the State de-humanized me. I did not have a name on my file, parents or brothers and sisters, they were all taken from me. I had a number on a file and a case worker that changed every now and again, there were no personal ties no trust or moments that had personal meaning. I was Avery / female / case number 5689 and I am sure there was some warning sign giving them the indication that I was a TROUBLED and DISTURBED child, maybe a skull and cross bones.

The families I was placed with were not lasting homes and most of them treated me like I was a stranger or that I had a sign on me that said "Danger proceed with Caution". I needed to escape this whole perception of me and find out what it was like to live like a grown up, be me without labels and put the true me to the test. So, I put a nap sack on my back and off I went into this real world.

Through my teenage years, I made the decision to hide my abilities. Things that came natural to me I had to hide. I needed time to educate myself about the abilities that I had, to know what they were and how to control them so that I did not have to be the outcast.

In the mid to late 70" s there was no internet putting a name on my abilities was hard let alone finding any books or knowledge of any kind. It would be many years before I would be able to put a label on it. It was Edgar Cayce, Silvia Brown, then John Edward who would give me the understanding of the abilities that I was born with.

The Clairs

The one thing that Edgar Cayce, Silvia Brown and John Edward talked about were the Clairs. These were psychic terms that gave me the understanding of who I am and they all connected to my senses. Clairvoyance (seeing), Clairaudience (hearing), clairsentience (feeling), clairsalience (smelling), Clairgustance (tasting), Clairtangency (touching), Clairempathy (emotion), Claircognizance (knowing) The only one I did not have was Clairgustance (tasting) That was ok though I do not know how I would have handled that, the rest of them were hard enough and since some tastes make me gag not having this ability was well appreciated.

When you are young and have all these things going on at once with no understanding of what's happening it can come off as very hard. I just accepted it as who I am, I never questioned it this was the way I perceived life and my world to be. Most of the world does not realize that this is the way we are born. Then life and free will get in the way and things change, we get mainstreamed. The judgement of others matters. The fallacies of the world become common practice. Religion demoralized certain aspects that we as humans were born with in fear of things they could not understand. These abilities gave each person their own power and only one person could hold that power and that was God. With all this in play humans became mainstreamed and these abilities that we all hold were buried deep within our soul. I was lucky in that aspect because no one could or took the time to mainstream me. I slipped through those cracks and essentially became me. I am very grateful for that aspect because it allows me to see things head on as real as it gets and I would not have it any other way.

The other things Edgar, Silvia, and John taught me was about my Intuition. I learned that gut feeling that sometimes would make me anxious or feel like I had to do something without knowing why, was my intuition and it was very important for me to pay attention to it. That all came with Claircognizance, that smack in your stomach when you know something but you keep doubting it trying to do things another way. I described that as my guardian or spirit guide herding me to another direction, or just telling me as it is. Trying to keep me from making bad decisions or even to bring me to some things that were good for me or meant to be. I must admit I did not always listen and doing things the hard way became a lesson well learned.

David

David was my husband's younger brother, his only sibling. He was in his early 20's when I met him, fresh out of school and full of adventure. That is exactly how David lived his life.

David had gone to cooking school and was an early success in his catering business. The first few years I knew David he had a partnership in a catering company in his home town. His clients boomed and he found himself with so many clients that exclusively wanted him. David always added that extra touch and care, that he made the decision to go on his own and he did, he created Café Merritt 8. That decision did not come without recourse. The company he was working for would stand to lose many clientele that David had built in the years he had been with the company David found himself in court, but that did not stop him.

David was very good at being a success. He knew business and the stock market and had a knack of making it all work for him. David loved the fast pace and competitiveness of the life he led. This way of life didn't leave room for bonding relationships and family. Holidays brought parties to cater and business meetings and the spring and summer weddings to dazzle. Seeing David at these times was a rarity but if we were lucky we would catch him for a brief lunch and off he went.

The times I did get to know David he was very open to who I was. He knew that I and my faith accepted all, we didn't discriminate, we did not judge. He knew of my abilities and at times would talk to me about them. He knew his faith held no place for him so he was in search of other avenues. It was important for him to find his place.

During these early years, David was on a path of self-discovery. Living life in the fast lane did not always give him time to find out who David was as a person so in1996 he took an adventure with his best of friends across the country. This adventure lasted 4 months and took him to all aspects of the country. He experienced the beauty of the bad lands in South Dakota and felt the energy of the majestic red woods in California and ended his journey on Mardi Gras partying the night away in New Orleans.

These months changed David forever, he knew who he was now. He had found himself in ways none of us had ever suspected.

When David returned home, I saw in his aura, in his energy that he was content, a great weight was lifted and life had just begun.

David had discovered a part of him that no one ever suspected and it took months before he had the courage enough to tell the family. One by one David told us he was gay thinking that it would change our outlook of him as a man, as a brother and Son. It did not. David was still the same person we loved with all our hearts. It did not change the way we looked at him and it did not change the fact that he was still a Man. To us he was more of a man for being himself and accepting the man that he is.

David did something for me as well. I was still learning some of the abilities that I had and what some of the signs meant to me and with his journey, it helped mine become clearer.

I always felt something different from David than I did with the family. I saw the mask like he was hiding but did not know for sure what it meant. I felt the different person that he felt on the inside, he was not the same person on the outside. I knew we all had that but this was different and I related and did not know why. His aura was always held tight and now he shined.

There have been many Ah-ha moments in my life as I learned more about me and this was one of them because now I saw it and now it was there for me to see and to learn from. Just like a new toy I would get I was anxious to play, to learn so I studied people more. I closed my eyes and felt their energy and learned more about the aura. I already had these abilities but now I was learning to expand them, I was adding knowledge and explanation to it all.

I was happy for David and I was happy for me as well. It clicked, this life is really a school a big earthly school.

The Guardian

In January 1998, way ahead of schedule a 3#9oz baby boy named Danial was born. He was the first grandchild born to the family and David's one and only nephew. The baby spent the next two months growing in the incubator and David visited regularly and held him when he could. Danial was a little bit bigger than David's hand. They bonded almost instantly. We knew then that David would be our first choice as his male guardian.

The person chosen for Guardian would have many duties along with stepping into taking care of our child in event of our death but it also stems beyond that. It asks the Guardian (God Parents) to guide and bring up our child in our values and faith until he was old enough to choose himself. To respect our beliefs and values and if need be to direct him to others who can educate him; such as; A Coven. To protect our spiritual belongings to pass them down to him when he is of age. (book of shadows, talisman, ritual tools). David embraced these duties.

Three months later we made David the Guardian of our Son. After a birth, welcoming ceremony to mother Earth, Father Sky and the universe a Wiccaning ceremony was planned.

The day of the Wiccaning ceremony as we rose bright and early to cleanse the area and prepare for our guests, I stood looking out the big picture window with Danial in my arms there in the front yard was a family of deer looking back at me that was a blessing from the universe but it was also a sign and we would see this again.

Many family and friends attended this beautiful and special ceremony. My husband's family were very apprehensive but attended any way. I don't know if it was because they wanted to make sure that Danial was not being sacrificed to the Gods or something silly like that, or maybe curiosity got the best of them and they needed to fill that with answers.

When the members of the Temple showed up to bless Danial dressed in robes and capes my mother in law and her sister went into a nervous dither. I tried to calm them by explaining the steps and what the ceremony was about but all they could comprehend was there were people holding Danial that were wearing black robes and carrying staffs and weapons with pentagrams around their neck. To them, in their world this was a sign of something dark and evil.

"Here ye! Here ye! It is time to gather round as we bless this newborn child." The sacred circle was cast and the elements were invited to honor and protect. The High Priestess welcomes all that were there to witness this right and assured all that this child or any child is not bound by any spiritual law to this Faith he will always have free will.

The ceremony was held in the front yard of our rented house that was set in on a dirt road but it didn't stop anyone passing by to slow down and take in the festivities with the Celtic music playing and the drums beating not even the birds that watched from above missed out as the Guardian parents walked Daniel to each element while he was bestowed wishes and gifts of years to come and given his sacred name that he would carry though his life until he chose to change it. The circle was opened and gifts and blessing were given by the guest. It was a joyous and special day, and David embraced it with all his heart. The rest of the family? Not so much. They excused themselves from this blessing celebration but not before they hid and stuck little Christian metals and crosses under dressing tables and cribs anywhere the baby would spend his time. I believe this made them feel a part of something they did not understand and just was not ready accept.

Part of me felt sorry for them. In their world that they had embraced and brought up their families to adhere to, had the perception that there was only one way to God and to them this was not it. This was unacceptable They had a real fear and that fear commanded the rest of this family's relationship towards me.

A Date with David

As I walked into the hospital room, all I could hear was the sound of the ventilator that was helping him breath. It was only a few hours ago, we got the dreadful call notifying us that David had been in an accident and he was now in a coma.

David was 39 years old and very much of a success in his life. He was loved by his family and a positive influence and best friend to his nephew.

David and I were never close, I thought he judged me for what I believed and the abilities that I had. I thought of him as reckless and lived life too much on the dangerous edge. My Son, was his nephew and Godson. As a protective mother, I feared at times that David's recklessness would eventually take my Sons life. So, in life, there was always this distance and firm arm between us.

As a sensitive, I was effected by the energy of the emotions that were building from my family as the fears turned to reality, of what had happened, it made my mind spin. I felt light headed and dizzy. "I know better than this" I said to myself "I should have shielded and grounded myself". I closed my eyes and clutched onto the crystal I keep safely in my pocket to regain my balance then I took some deep breaths. As my mind starts to clear, I heard a voice in my head say; "Trish, I am here, see me?" as I opened my eyes I was drawn to look towards my son and his father who were beside his bed looking at David lying there in total disbelief. There he was. It was that moment, my relationship with David began.

Through most of my life I had experiences that most people couldn't understand, I could see and talk to spirits. It was a natural gift for me, it didn't scare me or shock me, it was who I am and I embraced it fully. Though this was different, David was alive, he was just in a coma. I never experienced this before in this way. I thought to myself "Oh David, this cannot be real. "I can hear you breathing and see your heart beating on the monitor, your still alive. Although I knew of astral travel and I had read many books on how the soul can jump out of the body for the body to feel less pain while it heals. I had never experienced it or saw this happen myself, but I had that knowing inside, that knowing that told me this was real. David relayed to me that he felt no pain and his body was sleeping but he was indeed still alive. "You can hear my thoughts David?" I thought. "Yes" he replied. David didn't seem to be distressed or in pain. He had this feeling to me that he knew where he was and what had happened. I need to be by myself for a few minutes to get a grip and to wrap my head around all this. I needed to, I was going to have to be the strong one for my family.

The waiting room was empty, so I turned off the television that was showing the latest soap opera and sat down with my hands over my face and I cried. I knew that this was something I could not do in front of my family, especially my son.

My son Daniel just had his coming of age ceremony and David being his God-father was there to celebrate. The ceremony is a very personal and bonding experience for a child reaching puberty. The two-day ceremony consisted of God-father, father, grandfather and other chosen men who have important parts in his life that will help guide Daniel into manhood. Then he would get to spend a week with his Uncle and work in his restaurant and enjoy some fun and bonding times. That was the last time he saw David. Daniel was so excited about the time he had spent with David that he forgot to say Thank you when he dropped him off 7 days ago,. He forgot to tell him how much he loved him and needed him in his life, and it was weighing heavily on my son's mind. His last words from David was in a message telling him he wanted to see Daniel become a respectful and successful man one day. These words were on my mind as well this is my son and David was the world to him. Daniel was only thirteen I had to pull together. I had to help him through this. I could not expect his father to, David was his only sibling and youngest brother this is going to take all he had.

I gathered myself, dried my tears took one last deep breath and stood up to walk back in the room where David lay in a coma.

"So you believe me now? "I said. Aloud as I walked down the corridor" not expecting an answer. "I did not, not believe you before I just didn't remember;' I hear David say, 'and I am told I won't truly remember until it is my time to disconnect from my human shell but I am told it is not my time.

I went back into the hospital room to comfort my family. To give them hope. David thought he was going to make it through so now I have to convince them of this.

Through the next few days David and I had many conversations. I asked him to tell me of what happened that day he was eager to tell me.

David was on his way to visit a friend and former lover for his birthday. It was a beautiful Hot sunny summer day in July So David took his motorcycle. David loved riding his motorcycle. The roaring of the engine and the peacefulness of wind against him gave him the clarity and calmness he needed at times. He had lead a stressful life as a caterer and business owner of a restaurant and a cafe. He battled against the judgments of being gay, the emotions of coming out and the intensity of relationships, along with his addictions and illnesses that were a part of his everyday life. His motorcycle rides, even in the middle of the night, were David's solitude. That day, it was Dennis's birthday and he was the man who broke David's heart, but they were friends and he never missed a birthday.

So when David got out of work that day he road 40 minutes to the house that Dennis and he once shared to see him for his birthday. Dennis didn't expect him so he wasn't home. He waited a while and when Dennis didn't come home, he left a gift and a card on the table and started home.

It was right in the middle of rush hour on Wednesday evening and rush hour meant just that. Everybody! was in a rush in the City it didn't matter what time or night. David traveled the main strip and traffic was moving at a steady pace. As David was driving by a local restaurant bar an unsuspected car darts out over two lanes of traffic and makes an illegal left hand turn right into David and his motorcycle head on. That is when David left his body. "At first I didn't know what had happened "I thought it was a dream, but I still felt the pull, the strong energy to my body, so I knew I was not dead."." Why didn't you go back into your body?" I asked? "something told me not to, to wait." I saw the lights and the emergency crew working on me, I heard one man say I was not going to make it and that he thought I was surely dead. "David said, he stayed with his body. He saw the men working on him take something from him but I couldn't understand what it was that he took and he never brought it up again.

"I saw Dennis, pass by the accident on his way home does he know I am here?" I tried to yell for him but he couldn't hear me." At that time, I did not know nor had I thought about it. Dennis and David had moved on in their lives and David had another partner that had been in his life for at least a year. I felt the love energy and knew that he still loved Dennis. Dennis did come to see David and was having a hard time accepting what happened like all of us. It was clear that there was a deep love between David and Dennis but there were still open wounds that were never fixed. They believed that in time they could mend the wounds and their lives would find each other again. Now this was hanging by a thread.

David's prognosis was horrifying. A brain injury and he was on a ventilator to help him breath. His brain was swollen. To swollen to tell what was going to be. The biggest fear was David had no insurance and he had a secret. A secret that only few of us knew.

A few years back David had been in Brazil and as vein as David was, and he was with reason. I can personally tell you, David was a very good looking man, he dressed in the finest cloths, worked out on a regular basis and took very good care of himself. He could turn heads walking down the street from both genders.

Age and long stressful hours were creeping up on him. David was getting those horrifying, disgraceful looking lines. You know the things we call.

(*whisper*) wrinkles!!

So, David took a vacation in Brazil. While he was there, where no one would ever know, he got Botox.

David had money, he owned two business along with stocks and bonds and good financial sense. So, affording the Botox shots were not a problem those wrinkles were. Case closed.

The one thing about a foreign Country is that their laws on medical procedures and safety are more lenient than ours but David did not see a problem with this. Like many of us who just must have something he didn't think there would be any issue. Well 6months later he discovered he contracted HIV through the unsterilized needle. This could be an issue for David in his recovery and being that this was a secret even some family members did not know about, could lay heavily on decisions that would need to be made. I worried that not

45

taking his medication would cause him to develop AIDS and that AIDS would take David's situation to another level. We questioned whether we should ask the Doctor if they had tested him or if they had found records from David's other Doctors showing he was on medication I kept saying to myself with agitation and concern. David tell me what medication you were on so we can notify the doctors.

But David kept saying to me" No Mas!" although David was fluent in different languages, I was not. I kept seeing the don't do drugs sign and then right after that I would see the words No Mas.

Eventually I discovered it meant No more. And it was soon confirmed that David refused to continue taking medication for HIV. No Mas; No more.

Now you are probably wondering Did I know David had HIV? Because most people do wonder and are more than likely having an assortment of emotions on the thought even judgement. Yes, I did. It did not change anything. David was very responsible and took all precautions and no one, family, friend or lover ever contracted HIV from David. My son and him were close and I encouraged it without judgment. Like I said earlier, I only feared he was reckless. By living life in the fast lane. Living each day as if it were his last.

A month went by as David still lay in a coma. The news of David having HIV was brought to the family. With no insurance and physical signs, the decision was made to shut off the ventilator. David was breathing partially on his own. So we still remained to have hope that he would continue to breath on his own. I pleaded for this not to happen to give it some more time. But the news of David having HIV that was rapidly turning to AIDS and fear of quality of life, Orders were made to "Do not resuscitate" As they turned off the ventilator we were told to go to the waiting room. I was relieved they made us leave because I knew if David stopped breathing I would have to pick up my son and his father off the floor.

As we walk around the corner to the waiting room I hear David say to me, "hold him" I knew exactly what that meant I grabbed my son by the arm and brought him to a chair and sat him down. It was at that moment as I sat down next to him and turned towards my son. Daniel broke, all the pain he felt, the emotions of the past month, all of it came out loud and uncontrollable. I heard the pain in his cry It ripped through every inch of by soul, I, his mother who kissed away every booboo and healed his broken hearts could only hold him. His grandfather walked over picked him up and hugged him soon there were the three of them Daniel, my husband and my father in-law hugged in the middle of the waiting room. My father in law didn't say a word, how could he? David was his son.

As I look up at the three of them embracing, I see David there by the elevator, then he turned and went back to his room. The nurse came out and told us we could come back in again. I looked for David but I could only see his physical body lying there. No machines.

At 8pm when we left the room to rest, David had been breathing on his own and Edwin, David's present partner was by his side like he had been every night. My son Daniel grabbed David's hand and said "I am not saying good-bye, I love you. I will see you tomorrow" I looked again, I still didn't see David, there was a quietness, an emptiness that surrounded us now.

We left the hospital to get some sleep and would return in the morning. David was still breathing on his own so my son and husband felt hopeful.

I lie awake most of the night because I could not sleep. I try to talk to David. With no response. I toss and turn for hours. I must have fell asleep because at 3am I woke up in a panic, and the loud beating of drums in my head, louder and louder then stop! I cried NO! David NO! I begged. Please! David hold on! We are coming. Don't go. I saw him in a vision, not in spirit form like I did the past month. I put my hand over my mouth and cried, fearing I would awaken someone and they all needed to sleep. This was the first night they had slept this soundly. Then I heard it, a whisper in my inner ear this is not good-by Trish. Soon after the alarm goes off. We all get up and get ready to go to the hospital. There hadn't been a phone call yet from the hospital. Maybe I was just being over sensitive. This was the day we were going home to Pa anyway and I was nervous this time leaving so maybe I just over translated everything and David made it through the night. Everyone seemed to feel like we had made it through the night as we were getting in the car to go see David, the phone rang and the man who is the backbone of our family fell to his knees and the cry of distress I had never heard from him in the 18 years we have been together bellowed through the house.

David Died 6am that morning....

The three of us sat in a ball holding on to each other trying to comfort each other gaining enough strength for the 3-hour ride home.

David and I didn't communicate till weeks after that. David has been my constant Date ever since.

The ride back home for me was intense, the emotions and energy flowing through me was over whelming at times I felt like I was going to just collapse but I knew I could not. Silence had filled the truck, there was nothing to say. My family was in distress and lost, everything was so unreal to them. I felt their heaviness and pain and all I wanted to do was take it away, but I could not.

Many people feel being like me with the gifts I have would be so amazing and so glamorous and they want to have the same gifts but what they do not realize is that these gifts at times made me feel so helpless especially at that point in time.

My family has always trusted me and believed in me, this moment, this time it was personal and so over whelming for them that they did not have the strength and the mentality to believe in me and my gifts. I saw David as he comforted my family I felt his love energy and his life force. During this month, long process, I saw it but there was no way to help my family because to do so would take away the one thing they needed and that was hope. How was I to tell my family what the outcome was to be? How was I to tell my family that the decision they thought they made behind closed doors was not the decision that was carried out and the decision to let David go was made before they entered the closed room. I tried to tell my husband what I knew and what David had told me but he could not hear it. I felt desperate for him to see it, to hear what I was saying but he could not.

When they pulled the plug and David still was breathing on his own, I saw the look of hope and relief in my family's eyes, but I knew the decision that was made and there were no chances left. That decision gave away all hope. Before they stopped the ventilator, the family called their Pastor to give last rights incase David passed.

At that point I was having a hard time distinguishing voices from others thoughts and spirits talk, it was all jumbled nothing was making sense, I still could not see or feel David. I had to focus I was absorbing everyone. I needed to get away to regroup and ground myself. I had to leave the room and go outside, I felt like I was trapped in a box and my air to breath was slowly depleting. I quickly left and made my way outside of the hospital to the top open area in the parking garage, I found a quiet corner and gasped, at that moment it all came out. I sat down in a corner on the concrete and cried harder than I ever had in my life. I cried not for the loss that was happening but from the emotions, the helplessness and energies that built up in me and as much as I wanted to close myself off to these energies I could not because this was my family and I needed to help them, I needed to know how they were feeling. I cried and gasped for what seemed like hours, when I calmed I felt a presence in front of me and it was projecting this strong healing energy right at me. For a few minutes, I looked around and could not see anything, I wondered if it was David. Then

I saw him, from across the garage there he was, I got up and walked over to him "How long have you been here?" I said "The whole-time mother, I could not leave you by yourself, I know you and your breaking right now, you are carrying it all, I knew you needed to ground, I also knew you would not do it"

He was my oldest of four children, my son, and my rock and at that moment I did not feel alone anymore because he understood who I was. It was a moment we had both never been before, I was vulnerable and he was my strength and I let him.

The Silence

The days before the funeral were quiet. We all just went through the motions trying to prepare the best we could for the funeral. I knew that since we believed in different things about what happens at death than his parents, that we needed to do something in our own way. I was from the firm belief that funerals were for the living to help them process the transition from physical life, living to spiritual life, death. I knew if I prepared something for us to do it would help my family in their healing and would give us peace. I knew I could not tell my husband or my son yet of the experiences I had with David, they surely were not ready to hear it.

Music was prepared and a cleansing and passing ritual written. A poem was written from words that David was passionate about that expressed how he felt and had meaning to him and read at his church service to the congregation.

As we entered the funeral hall where David laid in a beautiful oak casket surrounded by bouquets of flowers. I could smell the flowers as we entered the room. I could see David in spirit making his rounds and greeting people as they gave their respects. I had a sense of relief and comfort seeing him, it had been days since I last saw or communicated with him and I had grown fond of it.

The emotions were high so I prepared myself with grounding and protection and carried my crystal in the pocket of my jacket and for this occasion I carried a crystal in each pocket so that I was not affected by the emotions of everyone who came and my focus and balance would be much steadier.

By the end of the night we were all just exhausted, we skipped the dinner with the family and headed straight to the hotel.

Good – Night I said to David.

The services the next morning began at the funeral home and went to the church and then to the cemetery. I had written a ceremony for us to do before the services and the arrival of others to the funeral home, so we needed to arrive earlier than the rest of the family.

I sage smudged the body in the casket, lit our candles then each of use formed a circle and held hands as we called in our elements and asked the guardians to guide our loved one to what some call heaven. We thanked the earthly realm for the body that carried his soul and now we give back to the earth. We played music and gave our blessing and messages to David. We said our farewells and release our circle.

We were all done when the rest of the family and friends entered the room. The Pastor arrived and said his blessing and closed the casket.

A Message From Me

A young Daniel bows his head, tears running down his face as the Pastor closes the lid. He looks up at his father who nods his head gently. "Be strong son" he says as they lift the casket up into the hearse.

"He was an Uncle, Brother, Son and Dear friend" The Pastor reads as he begins the eulogy.

The words of the Pastor were drowned out by Daniels own thoughts. He had stayed up all night thinking about all the lessons he learned from his Uncle, his best friend. Daniel wanted to tell everyone, most of all tell his uncle what he had learned from him and what he meant to Daniel. His last words to Daniel at the age of 13, made an impact in his life. David had called Daniel the day of the accident but Daniel had missed that call, and now he wanted to tell him, to show him. He wanted to make him proud. He wanted him to know he listened. Daniel wanted his words to be personal not just words and to have meaning, so he stayed up all night preparing.

The moment came, Daniel stood up and walked up to the Pastor, holding back his tears. he handed him his Red journal opened to the page and said, "My Uncle was my best friend, his last words to me was that he wanted to see me grow up to be a respected and successful man, and I want him to know I heard him, can you please read this?" The pastor nodded and took the red journal from his hands. "Thank you Pastor." Said Daniel.

The Pastor reads;

Dear David,

The last time I saw you, you were dropping me off after a week long adventure we had spent together. When I got out of the car I was so excited to tell everyone about the great time we had spent together that I forgot one thing, one very important thing, I forgot to say Thank you.

I am so sorry I never got to say those words to you, but I am saying them now. "Thank You, Uncle David. Thank you for being there and believing in me when I couldn't believe in myself, thank you for teaching me to grow up strong, and to set my goals, for anything is possible, but it takes work and focus. To remain honest and never Judge. Thank you. Always say Thank You.

As I sit here thinking of the lessons you taught me knowing each one has importance I am drawn to the words that impacted your life daily. A lesson and words that all here need to hear. These words I wrote from you Uncle David, they rang in my ears as if you said them to me last night.

The Pastor looked up and took a deep breath, paused and continued;

Do not judge me, I am who I am.
I may not love who you want me to,
But I do love just as deep and bonding as you.
I am who I am.

I may not have lived my life the way you think is
right,
But I lived life and experienced it, I did not let it
pass me by.
I am who I am, not much different than you.
My heart beats and my tears fall just as you.
Do not judge me.
I did not see me as better than you.
And I did not judge you.
I am who I am.
Do not judge me "......A message from me"

Daniel looked up and around the congregation, seeing intent faces as tears rolled down their cheeks. He knew that they were listening. Listening not only with their ears but with their hearts. The Pastor continued:

My uncle was a man, he cared about all people. As an owner of two food establishments he voluntarily served people in New York City during 9/11. He did fundraisers for Churches and Battered Woman's Shelters, He participated in feeding the homeless. He traveled the world to see the beauty in it... he brought me to New York City to show me the melting pot this country has with in it. He showed me what America does when it falls from grace, it gets back up and rebuilds. He taught me to view all in my eyes and heart as unique and individual and to always remember everyone has their own story, so do not judge.

My uncle was a man. He loved God and his country. My uncle was Gay. He did not Judge. And I loved him.

And although there are people who did not know who my Uncle was, what he had done for other. For he never asked for anything in return, judged him just by the person he loved.

When you took the lunch, he prepared and served you when you were hungry and broken at the sight of 9/11 when our country fell. Did it matter?

When he catered your wedding, and made your day a beautiful memory, did it matter.?

When he raised money for your church and shelter, did it matter? When you were cold and hungry and no food and he fed you, did it matter? Did he deny you his service because you were not like him? He was gay. Did it matter?

As the casket was lowered into the ground, Daniel heard the words whispered in his ear "*I am who I am, Do not judge me.*" "*Thank You* "Daniel knew then his uncle had heard him and That Mattered.

In loving memory of David; 1-21-73 to 9-13-11

Live to Ride, Ride to Live, always and forever in our hearts.

The Blessing and the Curse

David's passing was hard, like any other passing would be hard for anyone else but I stood steadfast to my beliefs in the afterlife and continued with helping my family through the reality of what had happened and educated them on what the journey to the Afterlife was so they could understand that David did not leave us his soul was still alive and he was still here and that we never truly die, that this is just another experience we go through and learn what we need to then move to our next journey. In many ways, each passing when you look back there is some lesson you yourself, through the pain has also learned. Some people get lost in the death and cannot see past it and miss the signs and the lessons left behind by our loved one and never embrace the journey.

Life for us was different now. I had to heal from the process, I was drained to the max and feeling helpless because I felt that what good was it having these abilities if I could not use them to help the people I loved. What good was it to know what was going to happen to see it happen and not be able to tell the people in your life because you were too close and they did not want to believe you and anything you said or tried to say was falling on deaf ears and heart, they just couldn't, they needed me to be wrong and this was my lesson.

As I regained my strength and focus I realized that my family did believe in me and as hard as it is being me when it is so close it is also hard on the ones close to me having someone like me. As they say "A Blessing and a Curse".

The Dream

David was silent for a while, it seemed like months before I had contact with him again and then he came to me in my dream.

The dream was not like my other dreams I had at night full of action and stories. This dream was just me, in a room waiting for someone to come in. The room was well lit and the walls seemed like they were a light blue in color. I did not see myself in this room I felt like me entering and waiting in a room. There was nothing around me in the room, no chairs, tables, couch or things on the wall. It was just a room.

I can feel an energy or a presence then I hear this voice that sounded like it was in a tunnel at a distance. It was different in tone, but I knew. "David" I said he said "yes" I felt myself wanting to say more but was not capable of it at that time. He told me he was ok and healing from his earthly life, then he said something that baffled me. "7/7 my immediate feeling was he was telling me someone would join him on 7/7 or was he reminding me of his accident? No, his accident was 7/6 I thought to myself. And that was the end of our meeting. When I woke up I knew what had happened and I was upset that I did not just ask some questions and talk some more but the conversation was not under my control and it is what it is. Now I had to figure it out. I asked my husband and other close friends and relatives to no avail.

Four years later, July 7th Doris, David's mother, my mother in-law was diagnosed with stage 4 lung cancer. 7/7, some people would not take notice of that not realizing that in spirit there is no time, time is an earthly concept and the afterlife has no time. There is no way of telling whether minutes, hour or years have gone by. Time is irrelevant, but with that it brings up a question I have not yet been able to answer and that is with this theory being truth for many how is it explained that spirits can predict dates and know anniversaries and birthdays are coming? Is it when communicating, the spirit must lower its vibrations and we must higher our vibration does that allow some earthly connection to time? This is something that has puzzled me for some time but have never put much energy into finding the answer until writing this book. I have always just trusted the information and who I am and left the other stuff to other people. I am open to anyone who has a reasonable answer for that question.

During those four years, I had also considered other meanings of the number trying to reveal what David might have been telling me so I decided to study numerology. I found it interesting that the number I was considering was the same number that was a birthmark on my left hand, and is still there to this day, the number 7.

The information below is taken from: permission given on site.

- (*www.sacredscribesangelnumbers.blogspot.com* :
  The Vibration and Energy of Numbers; Walmsley, Joanne;
  Sacred Scribe)

The number 77 is made up of vibrations of energies of the number 7, doubled and amplified.

Number 7 relates to inner wisdom and intuition, contemplation and discernment, understanding of others, inner strength and tenacity, learning and education, empathic and psychic abilities, endurance and determination, spiritual enlightenment, development and spiritual awakening and your divine life purpose. Number 7 also relates to good fortune.

Angel Number 7 tells of a beneficial time with obstacles overcome and successes realized. Your angels are happy with your life choices and are telling you that you are currently on the right path. You are encouraged to keep up the good work you have been doing as you are successfully serving your soul mission and life purpose that involves communicating, teaching, healing others and serving humanity in a manner that suits you best. You are encouraged to set a positive example for others and inspire them to seek their own passion and purpose in life.

Angel Number 77 is a very positive sign and tells you to expect miracles to occur in your life.

I found all this and the date of Doris's diagnosis very interesting and I felt validated. This and who I am has been my life purpose all along.

Doris

Doris was the monarch of her family and she ruled her roost. She had two sons, David and the man I married Daniel Jr. She had a very confident and strong personality and like most mothers she protected her family.

She was a well together woman, not a hair out of place and dressed to perfection always. I remember the nights I spent at their house I would awaken to find Doris sitting at her kitchen table, hair done, make-up on, earrings in dressed with a cigarette and a cup of coffee waiting to greet her family as they awakened from their night sleep. I would come down stairs hair in a tussle with sweatpants and a tee shirt not fully awake and stumbling over myself. No matter how she felt about me at the time she always greeted me with a warm hello and you always! and I mean always! Greeted her back.

Doris was a member of the local Lutheran Church and she did many projects for her church.

There were times we would have some deep discussions as to Religion and God but although she had some misgivings as to our beliefs and hoped one day we would feel that our beliefs were just a phase in our life and find our way to the church and God. As hard as it was for her she did what she could to respect our beliefs and way of life and at times would ask me questions. I do not know if she was testing me or if she truly wanted the answers and thought I could give them to her.

When young Daniel was born, we had made it clear that Daniel would be brought up in our beliefs and during his young childhood we had strict rules about his grandparents educating Daniel in their religious beliefs. We did not want to confuse him. As time went on we did allow Doris to take Daniel to church if she explained to Daniel that this was Her beliefs and we had ours and the world was full of differences and that was just the way it was.

As a family, we did not want to restrict our son from religion itself we just wanted the opportunity to instill our beliefs and values and when he got older he would have the opportunity to choose his own beliefs. He would have a very clear picture to his parent's beliefs and customs so if he chose to he could bring his family up the same way he was brought up.

Before Daniel was born we decided that we would not mainstream him so he could hold on to his natural gifts he was born with. We believed that religious beliefs are a personal choice and in the end, it all is the same bowl with different fish it is how you see it.

Through the years Doris would send us and our son her angel reading for the day as messages she hoped would be instilled she was still a little unsure we were doing the right thing and a bit worried that her grandson might end up a lost soul.

It was not until Doris was diagnosed that her thoughts began to turn. A week after diagnoses Doris started aggressive treatment, we got a call the following day of her first round of treatment that Doris had a hard time with treatment and was going back to the hospital for a few days. I knew then she was not coming home.

My son and I packed our bags and went to stay with pop for a week or so to help him adjust to Doris not being there. Being with someone for 48 years every day is wonderful until they are not there. We went to visit her pretty much every day except for one day out of the week when her treatments wore her out. By the second week I started hearing it and seeing the grey mist start appearing. Although I already knew she was not coming home there is always that little bit of unsureness where I question myself, but this was it, this was my sign the drums in the distance, they were faint but it is my sign that transitioning is beginning. Every time I visited I would stay back with her while others talked to the doctors or family members so that I could talk to Doris, to tell her I loved her no matter what we had battled through the years and I would be here for her to guide and help her. She understood that at times when her soul was listening and then there were those times when Doris was just Doris, like she had no business being in that hospital bed. I believe this is our free will trying to fight. Our earthly human body to fight to live on. The next day Doris would be erratic. Her sentences made little sense and her spoken memories were confused. Every day when I went to leave she would grab on to my hand with such desperation and beg me to get her out of the hospital and she swore that the staff were killing her, on one of our visits Doris scolded my son calling him David her deceased son for not coming to visit her more often, then in the next breath she asked him why is he not working we did not correct her we all played along.

As days went by Doris had less good days and she became very agitated. She would even deny that she was sick. On her good days, she made plans for that years Thanksgiving Day, it was the first-time Doris ever asked me or included me in making the Thanksgiving dinner. It meant a lot to her so I went along with her and planned our meal. We talked of her and Pop going to Niagara Falls a trip she had always wanted to take, but one thing after another got in the way. During the day sometimes when she felt alone she would make random phone calls, many of those calls I answered she thought she was talking to different people each time and I would just go with it because trying to tell her differently only agitated her "don't lie to me!" she would say. As Doris progressed she started seeing people from the other side and have conversations with them as we were in the room and get upset when no one recognized what or who she was talking about. 2 weeks before her passing she would everyday ask for things from home which we would bring her and she would stuff what she could in her pocketbook that she had on her bed with her at all times. I felt that was one of the signs of passing. The treatments got harsh and twice her heart stopped and they had to revive her, one of those times kept her in a coma for a full week. During that time, I could see the soul expanding farther outside her body and I could hear the drumming a little louder and more steady. Even when she was in the coma I would come and sit and talk to her telling her everyone was doing ok, they loved her with all their heart but they all understood if she needed to go walk with God and I would make sure that the Pop and the family would be ok.

Although I did not believe in God, Doris did, so I needed to speak what was comfortable and acceptable for her earthly mind.

7 days later Doris awoken from her coma, she was sitting up, laughing and having great talks of memories. I saw it in everyone's face, the treatments worked they thought, Doris had never been so alive, so awake. The hospital took her out of intensive care into a room. As my family was feeling hopeful, I still heard the drums louder. But I could not take this moment from them so I went along with it.

We left the hospital all in good spirits and went home for dinner and 3 hours later came back up to say good night and spend some more joyous time with Doris. As we drove to the hospital I sat in the back seat with my hands covering my face knowing that walking into that room they were going to find the not so happy Doris and I hoped for just one more night.

We walked in the room and there she was sitting up right like she was before when we left her. She greeted us and told us to sit, she began talking and talking about the things she had wanted for the family. She made us promise that we would get out of where we were and buy a house. My son she made him promise that he went to college and got a good education. She wanted us to make sure that the drama would stop in the family and that we did not let certain family members destroy what we all had. If we started to speak, Doris would get agitated and say" let me finish, listen to me" and we did. As I looked at her I saw her change. Her complexion, her face and skin. My husband looked at me from across the room and I knew what his eyes were asking me, and I looked back at him with sadness and nodded. That's when he knew she was not coming home.

I lay awake in the chair that night just talking to whoever was listening and hope someone was. Now, if I did believe in God at this point, what would I ask for? Do you pray for what is impossible at that stage in time, for Doris to get better when it is clear to know, that is not going to happen, or do you pray that her passing is easy on her and all the people who loved her? I am a realist and I cannot deny the process.

The phone call came in that next morning and I woke up to see Doris hovering over my husband not in physical form but in spirit. Doris's heart had stopped again they had brought her back again but this time the prognosis was not good, the cancer had spread more and was starting to enter the brain. We had issued 3 times for them not to resuscitate her and all three times they did, it was not her wish and this time she was in more pain and she was dying. We stopped all treatments and made her comfortable. We took turns holding her hand, we sang to her and read her on her last rights. When everyone was out of the room I held her and, kissed her cheek and said "Tootle Bee, Doris, I promise I got this and I love you" I watched her as she left her body and the room filled with others to greet her. At 4:05pm Doris walked with her God.

I knew through the weeks I helped Doris transition and that she is at peace now. I wear her locket and cross around my neck and I can feel her energy and speak with her often.

Just Passing through

There are so many ways a Spirit can contact us, with me, after my loved one has passed and their soul is no longer grounded to this earthly realm my first contact with them will be through a dream.

Many people have asked me how do I know the dream is a contact and not just a dream?

Every night when we go to sleep we have hundreds even thousands of dreams before we wake, most of which we do not remember but then there may be that one dream, the one that feels different and so real and it has left us wondering if it could be that loved one we miss so much. Each person can experience that moment in different ways, I can only tell you how mine was and hope it helps you some. First, you need to let go of any preconceived ideas and any fear you have of the afterlife. You did not fear them when they were alive in their earthly body why would you fear them now? If you are religious, that is wonderful hold on to that dear to your heart but do not apply that here it is not going to help you and in some beliefs, can cause you to miss the message.

Keep in mind that each spirit might have a different way as well, and a different feel'

When David came for his first afterlife visit with me as I mentioned previously, he came in a dream. His energy was familiar to me I recognized it from before at the hospital but the energy was slightly different, lighter. He had sense of purpose, like he was there and I was to pay attention and I did. To see him he looked healthy, David was young when he passed so age did not seem to change. We were in this space without walls it was bright but not like a bright sunny light like most people say they see. There was no other presence and I was not afraid. When he spoke his voice to me had no tone to it like it had when he was earth bound. I had a knowing that he was there and it was me and him for the first time since the days of his funeral. It seemed like only a few minutes we were together in my dream. When I woke the next morning all my emotions gave me the verification I needed. David had contacted me.

A spirit contact is all that and can be more and if you feel you had a loved one come to you in your dream than you can rest assured you did so pay close attention.

Spirits will often contact you in your dreams verses any other form. This is because it can bypass the ego mind that will block thing that do not seem of the norm. It will not dismiss through mainstream thought, such as life after death and the existence of it. Dreams are the easier path of communication.

When you have a visitation, it will feel very real and vivid and it is not easy to forget like regular dreams. The communication is not always in words but often telepathic hearing with your inner ear. The message is not long and dragged out it is to the point and direct. A warning is always followed by comfort, reassurance and love.

The spirit will appear healed and healthy all anger, disease and fear will be gone because they have now connected with what I call Source and others call the light of God.

There may be a glow about them or around them. You will feel comforted and at peace, you will not feel fear. You will be an observer not a player in the visitation. When you awaken

Autumn Rose

1959-2006
I had a dream last night my friend
You came to me and said Good-Bye
We sat there talking like old friends, that had
Done it many times before.
You said the Goddess had opened the door
And time had come for you to pass through, so
Much you have learned and now it is time
for you to learn more.

I had a dream last night my friend
You came to me and said Good-Bye
Life had been lived and time had passed
Since we talked, like the sisters we were in our hearts.
"Where did time go?" I said "and why did we let it pass by?"
"Life gets in the way." I said as I began to cry,

"It comes and goes and we never know when, where, or why."

I had a dream last night my friend
You came to me and said Good-Bye
I hugged you tightly and kissed you on the cheek
"Go in peace my friend until we meet again."

I will visit you in my dreams and talk to you as you pass by,
But life is constant and never ending,
So, in my heart you will stay
For this is not good-bye my friend
It is...
"Till we meet again."

With love and Honor
Trish Avery 2006

The early morning of February 5, 2006, I woke startled in a panic. I ran downstairs to find my husband who had gone to his early morning job up the street feeding new calves. I looked at the time it was 4:02 am. He will not be back for at least an hour yet.

I had a dream and it felt so real. Autumn was one of my very best friends and a High Priestess to a coven I was in. There had been issues with weather so I had not been down to see Autumn since before Thanksgiving.

Autumn owned a high-end hair salon and she was closed on Sundays so sometimes we would buy lunch and sit and have girl time. She and I would get together at every holiday and put together stuff for the local homeless. One year we set up in the city and served bowls of hot stew. Soup, Meatball sandwiches and corn chowder for the homeless and served them a hot meal on a very cold day. We were not able to do it this year, the city council got involved and blocked us from doing it, so Autumn and I collected money to get $10. gift certificates to hand out to the homeless so they could go to the local pizza place and grab some pizza and drink or a bowl of pasta with sauce. We also did hat and glove drives and Easter baskets and Easter Egg hunt for the homeless children. Autumn did very well financially so whatever we did not collect she would also donate so no one was left out. She hated to see people on the streets especially children.

I sat in the dark waiting for my husband to come home. I was worried and wanted to go see my friend. In my dream, Autumn and I were at the Book store where we loved to meet and sit in the New Age section looking at different books that might had recently come out and talk about them. I would recommend books that I had heard about to Autumn and she would do the same. We like discussing the last book we read. We were sitting there laughing and talking like we always did. We had a bond like sisters did. Then Rose stood up, raise her arms in Goddess position, she turned to face me and said that the Goddess is calling her, she had done what she needed to do here, she needed to go learn more. I was speechless as she walked toward the veil. I ran to her and held her tight and kissed her on the cheek. I will visit you in my dreams my friend. I told her to go in peace till we meet again. 5:45 am I heard the truck come down the road, the truck door shut. I ran to the door and opened it as soon as he reached it. "Daniel, I had a dream, I need to go see Autumn"," today Daniel!!" Even though Daniel said we will go if it eased my mind. I still was not comfortable, I still had a bad feeling in my gut.

As I walked into the living room I looked up at the clock and it was 6:05 a.m. I went to the phone and went to pick up the phone to call Autumn, she is a early riser and all I needed to do is hear her voice and I would be ok and Autumn will just laugh at me for over thinking again. Just as I reached for the phone the phone rang. Who is calling this early in the morning? "hello? Trish?" "yes" There was a pause that seemed like a long time then I heard a sob and his voice, "Trish this is Evan, I don't know how to tell you this" I began to cry, Evan was Autumn's Partner, they had been together for 4 years and were talking about getting married. Through his sobs he said "Autumn, I tried to save her, she just, just started gasping, there was no warning, I pulled over on the highway and yelled for help, no one would stop. The cars were going so fast they couldn't hear me. She died in my arms, she is gone Trish. All

I could muster up for words were, "I know." For what seemed like 10minutes there was nothing only the sound of sobs on the phone. Then, Evan spoke again, "You know? "How? "She passed at 3:51 am, a few hours ago and besides the family, you are our first call." "Autumn came to me in a dream and she said Good-Bye, I watched her go. I was hoping it was just a dream, my inner knowing told me otherwise." I told Evan of my dream. I truly feel that for at least the hour we spent on the phone talking about my dream helped us both find some peace and get a better grip on the reality that we will be enduring the next few days. Autumn was a Mother, soon to be grandmother and just as importantly a High priestess to our Modest Coven, it was our duty to up hold Autumns respect and honor, by consoling our group of family and we did so that night by gathering us all together at Autumn's salon. Being in the salon which was part of Autumn's house without hearing her voice and laughter just did not feel right. How could a woman like Autumn who is so strong and so respected just die like that? Although many people were mingling and chatting amongst themselves there was something missing, you could feel it. This was not right, everyone was so formal, this did not feel like the same group of people, no one knew what to do or how to act. This free-spirited group of people were so closed off. I Could not take this rigged feeling. It was like they were just putting on a show and waiting for Autumn to come through the door and say "Gather round the ritual will soon begin." That was not going to happen not today, not tomorrow, not again. We needed to get it all together, we needed to do what is right. I am the maiden to the High Priestess of this coven, so I needed to step up. I went and found Evan, "come with me Evan, now." We both went to address the coven. Evan and I stood before our coven with blank faces and said "grab a candle and let's go." Everyone grabbed a lit candle that was placed all over the salon and followed me to the porch. The porch looked out over an in-laid stone circle in the back yard that was all fenced in for privacy. I few summers past, we all helped Autumn lay the stone and turn it into our sacred space. After all the stone was laid and the circle was ready we all blessed, consecrated and empowered the circle and the space for ritual and magic. As we look out upon this circle, we all started a light, faint humming. Then with our candles we made our way down the stairs to the circle. Our humming got louder and louder as we walked. Someone carried salt, someone consecrated water, and someone else with a sage stick. The rest carried tekke torches and candles. Evan a sword and I carried Anubis. Anubis is a God of the afterlife and was known to usher the souls to the afterlife. When I went to pick up Anubis from the windowsill in which it had sat there was a dragonfly sitting upon his head, that was my sign that Autumn was there with me.

Our humming turns to chants as the candles were placed around the circle, and torches lit at each element, earth, air, fire, water, spirit. I placed the Statue in the center of the altar. The gate to the west was opened. The chanting turned to singing. Singing of the Goddess. I spoke the invocation of Anubis as they all lightly chant "take me home". When the ceremony was done, we stayed in the circle as we all told memories of Autumn and blessed her spirit. We cried and held each other. When we opened the circle, and looked out among the rest of the mourners they were all on the porch looking down upon us. At that moment, we were all one.

"I had a dream last night

The Accident

My abilities were constant and only got better as I grew up because I managed to get through the cracks without being mainstreamed. People were either afraid of me, did not believe me so they always tested me then ran, or just ignored my abilities like to acknowledge them would open a Pandora's box that they had no idea what to do with once opened. Through the years, I had kept my abilities to myself. Only a hand full of people knew what I was capable of and they did not even know the full extent of them. I never had too many friends, it was easier that way and to be honest that did not at all bother me. Less judgement and less issues. The friends I did have I had to trust with the basics never fully showing all of me. My own husband and children did not even know fully my extent either fearing that they would not see me as me but me as a freak or a monster. Until the accident.

It was early in the morning and I had an early shift that

day. I worked as a security guard at a big corporation a few towns over. It happened to be middle of July so the sun was just beginning to rise over the horizon when I left for work that morning. I heard a familiar voice in my head telling me to beware, the voice was of a close friend at the time who was home in his bed sleeping at that time, so as most people would do I just brushed off the warning.

As I came around a slight corner I saw something blocking the street that looked real, and in solid form blocking the entire road and as I avoided hitting it I swerved and ran over the embankment and hit a tree. Needless; to say, I was taken to the hospital and did sustain a concussion. It took a few weeks to recover, but when I did, I noticed something different about me, I even felt different. I had no control over my abilities and now no secrets. The only thing I could do was keep my emotions under control and that was going to be very hard because I was also feeling extra sensitive. I felt like Aunt Clara on bewitched with a cold. I heard voices and saw spirits as they passed through regularly, there was no seeing just some. If I got angry or dramatic in any way things would fly off the shelves. I knew I could do these things before but I kept that under control. One day while my husband was at work, My son who was 7 at the time was in the kitchen and I had gotten angry about something and there went the soda bottle keys, and some books flying off the table. My son screamed and ran and hid. I tried to calm him but now he was afraid of me, just as well at the time because the more I got upset the more the books and other objects flew off the shelf. My husband came home from work that day and I was in a panic when he opens the door he found me sitting on the floor crying, he was in shock as to the mess. My son heard his father's voice and came out of hiding. I knew then I had to do something. I had to control my emotions, at least until I could figure out what to do. So, I started making Chamomile tea and using rescue remedy regularly so to keep me calm. The next few weeks I worked on my chakra's which

I call my balancing system and meditations and finally after a good 6moths got myself pretty much under control.

Many of you reading this are thinking; ok you had me up until now, now you sound crazy. I guess to most I do, but what had happened is that the accident threw everything off balance, like hitting a switch on the volume button of a television and getting stuck there. All my abilities increased and I couldn't shut them off. When my concussion healed so did the enhancement of my abilities. Although going to work and trying to maintain some sort of normalcy was very challenging at best but at my job I was at that point put on second and third shift in the scale house so I just had minimal contact with others, except for the drivers that came through and that contact lasted 5 minutes at the longest. The other part of my job was riding around the plant in the company truck checked different parts of the plant. so, my job at that time was a benefit for me.

In the long run, I do believe that the accident helped me immensely. It brought what I was hiding out into the open so that I could get help with controlling it and keeping secrets from your family is so stressful, also by doing that it brought out some more abilities and strengths that I have today.

If it was not for that accident I would be in many ways alone, like I had been all my life and what good is my abilities if they are locked away. What good is life if you cannot live it free and be who you are. There had been many times in my life that I felt that taking my own life would have been the right thing to do. I said to myself many times that if my family ever saw me as a freak I would end my life. Then that one day when I scared my little boy and mortified my husband it was that moment I always feared. The look of disbelief, the look of fear on their faces was what I dreaded and wished would never happen, but it did, that day but after that shocking moment, when everything settled my husband just reached out and held me and told me it was ok and we would figure it out.

The relief gave me comfort and a new freedom then laughter filled the room.

Going out in public became very challenging because even though I had balanced out my vibrations that were linked to my abilities, I was more sensitive than I was before the accident and being at the mall or in a chaotic environment drained me and created some emotional mood swings than ever before. I got to the point that I hated being around people, at times the energy made me physically ill. I limited myself to minimal energies while I did research to find out how I could protect myself. There had to be something, I am not the only one in the world with these kinds of abilities, we all have them just most people get mainstreamed in believing it is not natural. I did not want to be like that, these abilities are who I am to take that away would take away me, I would not be able to exist.

I read books on grounding and shielding to see if I could find other techniques or Ideas that I had not used before that might help me now. This was way beyond the smudging and shielding techniques I did regularly. I read books on other mediums and sensitives who lived with some of the same things I did. I talked to others in the metaphysical field. I even took some classes that I thought might help. I did daily cleansing and shielding to get by but I needed something stronger. Then I found a technique that seemed to make sense to me. I learned that we as humans, absorb energy through our solar plexus if you were to cover up the solar plexus with a bandage it could not absorb the energy. So, I thought to put it to a test. I wrapped my solar plexus with an Ace bandage, did my cleansing, grounding and shielding rituals and went to a crowded area, The mall. I found it to be very helpful. I did not hear anyone's thoughts and feel their frustrations. I did not feel sick or anxious. I took some time to venture into some stores, shop and have lunch. For the first time, I felt what others called normal felt like. This feeling took much time to get used to and rather frightening. Being who I am was my protection. I knew when someone was coming up from behind me, I knew what they were thinking now I had to be aware. Although this seemed so horrible to me it turned out to be a good thing. I finally got to gain the control I needed to live a normal life or should I say to live like most people. To touch and hug without being totally overwhelmed and not know the other person's secrets. I learned how to turn it on and shut it off. I could be in the public eye and function without the world knowing who I am.

The Hotel

For three years, I worked as a housekeeper at a Historic Hotel in my town. The Hotel was built in the late 1800 but had changed hands and modernized to suit the times.

Although I lived right down the street from the hotel I had never been in the hotel part of it just the bar area and the dining room for dinner. As a housekeeper, my job entailed cleaning the bar and the dining areas as well as the rooms in the building.

When I first started, my first day was training. As we were in the dining room and I was being shown what had to be done in that room. The owner came in and he had to fix something in the vents, as he was leaning over into the vent with his handyman next to him I see this ghost of a manly figure leaning over them with his hands behind his back looking at what they were doing, it looked to me like this ghost was trying to find out what they were up to. He resembled the guy on the chance cards in the game monopoly and seeing him made me smile.

It was dark in the dining room because the sun had not come up yet and just dim lighting was on at the time, but an hour or so later when I came back into the room to continue my job checklist I saw on the wall next to the piano a portrait of the original owner of the hotel and I will be diddley swig-gets if it was not the spit image of the ghost I saw earlier that morning. Now my interest in this place was more than just a job it was an adventure for me.

I did not know any of the history of this wonderfully exciting place and that is the way I like it. I do not like to be able to pre-judge any of the things I see, experiences I have or information I receive. I get information first and then I do research to get verification of what is going on. During my 3 years, I encountered many spirits of the Hotel. The dining room did not just hold one spirit, it held a few. The next one that I had contact with is the Madam. When I saw the Madam, she had a very commanding energy like that of a debutant, she let me know that she was the Madam of the brothel, I have never found any information that the hotel was a brothel but I do believe that a madam ran her business through that hotel.

There were times I would smell a talc type smell of flowers and then I would see her there in her corset type garment. I did not hear her speak much just a cordial hello to let me know she was there. Her presence was strong at times and very well known by me when she was present.

The Piano man

The Christmas season was upon the Hotel and it was the employee's duty to decorate this old but elaborate Hotel for the holidays. The hotel still held the essence of the years past. Christmas carols we still sung around the Christmas tree summoning Santa and Mrs. Claus for all the little children. In years past the dining room of the hotel would have a person playing holiday music at the Piano. One day while I was cleaning the dining room I was startled by a man standing at the entrance of the dining room. For just a second my mind thought about how he may have gotten in the front doors were locked until 11 am and it was way before that. But I was brought back by the man's words. "I am here to tune the Piano, he said. he was carrying a leather bag that resembled that of a tool bag so I did not hesitate and went into the kitchen to alert someone of his presence and to find the hotel assistant to help this man with his duties. When I returned to the room again with the hotel assistant the man was gone and all the doors were locked from the inside. I just looked at the assistant and shrugged, laughed and walked away, what could I do? I held a reputation of being a witch so of course this incident became the talk of the hotel that day. I never saw that man again after that. I often questioned myself wondering how I saw him so clearly and heard his voice like it was of this lifetime. The only conclusion I come to is that the light was dim, my focus was on other things but my senses were high. It is often thought that spirits will only be seen in a misty transparent form but this is not always the case. If I had stopped and paid more attention I would have seen that this man was dressed in period clothing and his style was peculiar of the time. I would have paid more attention to the time of morning and the weather outside for it was snowing out. He had not any snow on him and no wet footprints on the floor.

I continued my day and let the talk of my presumed delusion to continue for that is not something that I am a stranger to.

The Dining room was not the only place that the spirts were occupying some were just passing through others were there regularly and everyone had their own opinion why they were there.

The Third Floor

On the third floor, there was a woman dressed in period clothing with her hair done up in a bun. It appeared to me to be of Victorian Era. She wore a long dress with some lace as trim. The waitresses had to go up there for supplies and were often afraid of her fearing she would harm them. Spirits never scare me unless it is to startle me. I am personally more afraid of a live person popping out at me than I am of a spirit, but it is my belief that most people fear what they do not know and religion has played a big part of that. They are taught to believe that the dead that lurk can hurt or even kill the living. As long as I have been here in this lifetime not once with all my experiences have I ever been harmed by a spirit or fought demons that were of pure evil or out for some revenge on the living. Therefor I did not fear spirits but explaining that to someone else was not an easy task and It was not my place to contradict what they believed, each person had to find their own discovery. What I did discover is that the woman on the third floor is a residual spirit that repeats her last day they have no awareness of the presence of the living or see them. They just pass by doing the same thing and they are seen at different times. I believe that this third-floor spirit was this type of spirit. She never left the third floor in the three years I was there and she was seen mostly when the veil between the worlds were thin enough.

In experiencing these spirits in all the ways that I have it is my belief that anger and intense emotions are of the human body and when we shed the body we only have universal energy that is our soul. Anger and intense emotions come from the brain and the chemical reactions we have that ignite them. When our spirit leave our body and our spirit and soul reunite as one we are part of that universal energy earthly emotions have no effect. We carry the lesson of this lifetime but not the burdens of it. This topic I will go into further in another book.

Little Jimmy

Not all spirits are residual, some interact. Like who I called little Jimmy. I cannot say that is his name when he was here among the living it is just a name that I felt compelled to call him. Little Jimmy was around the age of 6 or 7 when he passed away and for some reason like to remain in the hotel. He moved freely from room to room playing little tricks on unsuspecting people who worked or stayed at the hotel.

On occasion when I was working in the rooms upstairs especially one certain room I will call 42, he would like to sit on the bed and watch TV. At first I did not see him just felt his presence and he would do certain things for my attention. One of the things would be to turn on the TV when no one was in the room. When I would go in the room to change the bedding and turn off the television I would put the remote control on the night stand and leave the room to put the sheets in the laundry room and get a fresh set. I would come back into the room and the television would be on and the remote on the bed. If I turned off the light I would come back in the room with the light back on. When I was scrubbing the bathroom, Jimmy would like to shut the door on me. After a while I started talking to him and treating him like I would my grandchildren. "Jimmy, open the door back up please, I do not want it closed." I would say and go back to my work and he would open the door back up. "Jimmy put the remote back where I had it "and I would show him what the remote was in case he did not know and leave the room, when I came back it was on the night stand. This went on for many months then I decided I would bring in some toys like a ball and some cars and blocks. When I had the opportunity to clean that room or the room was not occupied I would put my toy in the room leave the door open and walk away to do the other rooms. It took a few times before there was any interest in the toys. Using one toy at a time, then one day I walked into the room just to check and the cars were on the floor lined up one behind the other not on the dresser where I had left them. There was only me on that floor or In and out of the rooms so I said Happily "So jimmy liked the cars, I will bring them again the next time." And I did. He played with balls and cars we even did the flash light trick. "turn the flash light on if you liked your toy today" I would say. One day I brought in a set of magnets thinking he might enjoy playing with them, I heard the magnets clash together once and I went into the room and I felt that Jimmy had left. I do not know what it was that made him leave but it was a month before I heard or felt Jimmy again after that. When he did come back I was happily surprised He let me know by getting my attention doing his original antics. Jimmy knew I was not afraid of him and soon I got a glimpse of this little boy with shorts and suspenders. He had a smell of smoke about him and his face was tarnished so I assumed he was either in a fire of some sort or he was of the coal miner's era, we never disgusted how he died I just like playing with him. He did not feel sad and when I did hear his voice it was only of a playful giggle. I no longer work at the Hotel but I often wonder about little Jimmy and if he will find another playmate.

The Honeymooners

I think one of my favorite stories at the hotel was the one I called the honeymooners.

It was 4th of July weekend and the hotel was going to be busy that weekend and the gas industry was in town and going home for the holiday so all the rooms needed to be cleaned so the holiday travelers could check in for the weekend. I had 12 rooms to do and like always I started at the end of the hallway and worked my way up. I had stripped the beds in 4 of the rooms and had to hand carry the sheets to the laundry room down the hall and grab the sheets I needed to make the beds. As I started down the hallway I see someone that looked like they came out of the last room at the end of the hallway. It was one of the suites a beautiful room with a Victorian deco and big windows that looked out over the town. It was the last room in the hotel so it had much privacy.

I was the only housekeep doing these rooms so I knew it

was not another housekeeper so I yelled down the hallway "Hello can I help you?" no one answered the person appeared to walk around the corner in the direction of the balcony. I continued down the hallway just as I turned the corner I saw a woman with a sling wrapped around her arm, she said she was here to meet her husband they come up every year for their anniversary. She wanted to sit and wait for him on the balcony and asked if I could open the door for her she was hurt and could not, I said yes and proceeded down the hall to help her, she had ducked back into the alcove by the balcony to wait for me to open it. When I got down to the end and turned down the alcove to open the door there was no one there. I checked the balcony porch, no one there. I was puzzled but did not have time to spend figuring it out I still had many rooms to do. I went and dropped off the dirty sheets in the laundry room and grabbed some more. While I was in there I checked the reservation sheet to see what time the honeymooners were to check in figuring I would do that room next since it was obvious the woman was already here, where I do not know. But sure, enough Mr. and Mrs. Anderson 45th wedding anniversary and flowers were coming from Mr. Anderson to put in the room as a surprise for his wife. Well at least I was not crazy. As I went to go back with the sheets to the previous rooms I was compelled just to look out on the balcony so I walked over and just glanced on the balcony and there she was sitting peacefully in the rocking chair on balcony, A few minutes later the other maid came up from downstairs and said I could wait on the honeymoon suite because there was a cancelation. I told her there must be a mistake Mrs. Anderson is already here and sitting in the rocking chair on the balcony, I directed the other housekeeper to the balcony and there was no body there. The housekeeper informed me that Mr. Anderson had called and told them his wife was in an accident last evening and has passed away just that morning. I could not help but cry for the couple and when the flowers came that morning I placed them on the table on the balcony where Mrs. Anderson sat that morning.

It is amazing for me to be able to see this kind of love. The Andersons had celebrated their anniversary every year and were planning on doing it again this year but a tragic accident happened and the celebration had to be canceled but Mrs. Anderson needed to finish her journey. To be in the place where they began. It is a beautiful thing. Love truly never dies.

This is where I love being me.

Attention!!!

When the gas company hit our area, it brought much business to the merchants in the area especially the Hotels. Companies would book rooms for months at a time for their employees to live. Some brought video game systems for their off time and many brought memories from home to comfort them while away from their families.

One of the rooms house a man that I knew just by his requests and the way he kept his things that he was retired Military. He wanted his bed sheets changed daily, he wanted them tucked in without a crease" nice and crisp" as he would say. He would hide a coin in the sheets so he would know if the sheets were changed or just made and we only found that out because the message of daily changing did not get to one of the other part time housekeepers and she made the bed instead of changing it and he went straight to the owner he then became my room to take care of exclusively and when I was off the other fulltime housekeeper. He kept a bible and a small flag on his night stand. His bathroom products were all placed strategically nice and neat. We needed to make sure that everything if moved was put right back into place exactly and precisely how he had it.

This man's sternness intimidated me and every time I went

into his room I felt like someone was watching over me. Most people would more than likely conclude that my feeling of someone watching me stemmed from the intimidation I felt of this man, but being the person that I am with the gifts that I have I knew differently I just had to bring out more of the spirit who was watching me, I knew it was not any of the spirits I had encountered in this hotel before and I knew it was not just lingering energy from the man that was living in that room the past month. So, I started talking to the spirit every time I entered the room. I would introduce myself and say hello, and talk about myself. I even asked questions like why are you here? Do you know the man who lives in this room? Then one day after asking the same things for about a week or a little more I hear "he is my father" I stopped and turned around and there before me stood a soldier in uniform, combat greens. Ok let me add here, yes this is me and yes I have done this all my life it is just who I am but there are times that you stop in your tracks and are startled and this was one of those times. I am already intimidated cleaning this room making sure every little thing is perfect and suddenly here he is, the spirit I felt and have been coaxing for a month to speak to me. Well he did. "I need you to tell my dad it is not his fault and to go home" and then the soldier was gone. Now this is where I crumble. It is one thing to see what I see and hear what I hear but to go up to a perfect stranger, this man particularly and say "Well sir, your son was here this morning and he wanted me to tell you it was not your fault. And to go home" I envisioned many different outcomes of what could happen here from being decked to losing my job being totally humiliated but not one of those scenarios had a happy ending. As much as television mediums or weekly programs are seen going up to people and saying "hey, your mom wants you to know she is ok and loves you." Is not as easy as it seems and I could never picture myself doing that nor did I have the guts. From that day forward this soldier made his presence known. I would see him guarding his father's room when I came in for work in the morning and when I went up to clean the rooms he was there, and he would follow me telling me I needed to tell his father his message.

The soldier had died in action and his father was carrying this guilt that if he had not allowed his son to follow his footsteps and join the army he would be alive today. "I was proud of my dad, I looked up to him, I wanted to be like him. It was my choice and my duty." His father had taken a job with the gas company that took him all over the country and left his mother home and she needed him. His father would go home a few weeks out of the year but spent most of his time on the road sending his wife money for the bills. His dad needed to go home and spend his days with his wife.

I made a promise that I would do it the next time I saw the man if I saw him because he was gone before I got there in the morning and back after I left and I had no Idea what this man even looked like. One morning two weeks later a storm came in and all the gas men were grounded and would be for a few days. Most of the men decided to take an early weekend and go home to see their families, so I assumed my military man would leave as well after all he did leave on weekends, I do not know where he went to he did not go home. I found out later he went to the nearest VA facility and volunteered his services and helped in churches. I feel that helped him with his pain. This day, when I knocked on his door before entering, something we always did. He answered the door. What did I do? I would love to tell you I gently told this man all he needed to hear. That his son was ok and it was not his fault and that his wife needed him at home. Sorry to disappoint you but I did not, I stood there frozen with headlight eyes stumbling over my words. He chuckled at the sight of me and said "come back in an hour to clean my room, and make it quick cause I am going out to breakfast and when I come back I do not want to wait." I did as he asked. I did not see him come back I just noticed the do not disturb sign hanging on his door and who am I to disobey? I had missed my chance to give him the message from his son. This weighed on me I had to tell him, I felt like this was my duty and it was so important. The hard thing is that many people due to their own beliefs do not believe in spirits or life after death so anything you tell them only adds humiliation to the message giver. The military man's whole demeaner was of someone whom you did not want to get a lesson in humiliation from. I needed to remind myself that my gifts source is universal I needed to let go of my ego and do what my gifts were intended to do. As I left work that day I knew that I had one more chance to tell Military man the message his son had imposed upon me. I also knew that if I did not deliver this message it would haunt me forever. I had to tell him. When I got home I sat down and proceeded to write The Military man a letter.

Dear Military Man:

I would like to introduce myself, my name is Trish. I have been for the past few months the housekeeper assigned to your room. Out of respect for you I will not hold back or beat around the bush as to the reason for this letter. As a person, I carry many gifts that give me the ability to see, hear and speak with spirits. This may not be a belief of yours but it is who I am and for the past few weeks I have had a contact with a gentleman who calls himself your son. He said he was killed in combat and although a retired military man yourself and someone who is aware of the casualties that being a military man holds, you have blamed yourself for his death, feeling if you had not encouraged your son to enlist then he would be alive today. Sir, your son tells me differently he tells me he has always held you in high respect and looked up to you and wanted to grow up to be the man that you are. He said enlisting was his choice and it was one he made with full awareness and honor. His death was not your fault and he does not want you to bare that burden. He died serving his country and he wants you to honor that. To go home and be with his family, his mother needs you. He will always be with you.

Sir, I know all this seems to be on the weird side for you *and I apologize if this has upset you, your son has been very adamite that his message get to you.*

With all respect

Trish

I placed the note on his night stand hoping that I would not receive backlash and that this man who clearly missed his son and loved him so much would find this note as a gift and give him closure.

The next day when I went to work the Military man had checked out and his note to me was Thank you I am going home. God, Bless you Trish. With a tear in my eyes I whispered Thank you. I felt the energy in the room neutralize and I felt proud to have been a part of this wonderful thing and to help a family after many years to be able to help them heal and know that the love for their son and his for them never dies.

*"Sometimes in tragedy we find
Our life's purpose, the eye sheds
A tear to find its focus"*
                                    -Robert Brault-

Abagail

Sept 11, 2001 was, for our nation one of the biggest and most tragic days in History. That day touched every single person in this country.

We had just moved a year prior from Connecticut where we were born and raised to Pennsylvania where the ends justified the means a bit more. Rents were cheaper and houses were a steal compared to the average Suburban home in Connecticut. With a family to take care of and barely making ends meet, making the move just seemed to be the only option at the time. I had been a little apprehensive about moving, I had friends and family and I was moving to an area where I was starting all over again and worst of all my husband was going to be commuting back in forth to Connecticut for work till he found something in Pennsylvania. It had not taken long before he got tired of being away that he found something in Pennsylvania and our life started to settle down a bit and we started to see some of our old friends again. They would come up to visit and we would go back home, it was the best of both worlds.

One of my closest friends Tony had gotten a job in the city and called me one day to tell me that he had achieved his dream and just got promoted and literally moving up in the world, a few floors up in the towers in New York City. Tony always had such a care free personality like he just went with the flow of life moving towards his goals smiling without a stress in the world.

We laughed and talked for a few hours, he looked out his high-rise window and described in detail what it looked like and how beautiful it felt to him seeing all those lights. Before we knew it, it was time to hang up. We set a Date for Oct 8, 2001 to meet in Connecticut and we would have a long lunch and catch up on all the latest stuff we were both missing out on since we both had moved away. I was excited and could not wait, it had been a few months since I had seen him, and Tony was very special to me. We called each other with our ups and downs and joked with each other to get a smile. Tony was a good prankster he always like to end the day with a smile.

.' Good Night Tony" I said but I felt uncomfortable, I did not want to hang up, I felt like something was wrong, I had a vision of him standing in front of A big window looking out and the window is black and he is looking at a big ball of grey cloud, or dust coming at the window as he stood still watching it and poof!! It is gone, him the window everything blank. That was Sept 10, 2001.

The next morning, when I woke up from a restless night I felt anxious and I did not know why. Tony and the vision I had still haunted my mind it was something I just could not shake. I grabbed my son out of his crib and brought him into the living room and I turned the Television on so my 3 ½ year old son could watch his cartoons. As I got his breakfast ready I thoroughly went through my conversation with Tony and recalled my night wondering what this feeling was all about and why I still had it. When Daniel's breakfast was ready, I went into the living room to get him and I saw it, the towers were attacked, I put my hand over my mouth as to hold back a scream as tears welled up in my eyes. I fell to my knees in terror. I could not hold back the heartache, the shock and the disbelief of what just happened. I felt it, the loss and the pain, not just mine the Nations, it made me weak and sick to my stomach I ran to the bathroom to throw up. I sat back on the bathroom floor as I hear the pitter patter of little feet running towards me calling my name. "Momma" Daniel said as he came in and gave me a hug. He never saw me cry and it was obvious he felt my pain, it all happened so fast that I had not had the time to shield myself. Danial sat on my lap while I gathered myself and my thoughts together. I needed to pull myself together and find out what had just happened. I picked up Danial from my lap and carried him back to the living room and turned on the local channel. The News said that both the towers were hit by an airplane and they feared mass casualties. My mind was racing and I could feel what seemed like the emotions of the world. I went to my room and found my black bag that contained a big clear quartz crystal that I use to clear energies it would help me balance and bring me back into focus, I needed a clear head. I opened the bag and grabbed the crystal and held it close to my chest and then my third eye I took some deep breaths in and out. I started to feel better so I took the crystal and scanned Daniel to help calm him from my anxiety. Now I was ready to hear more, I kept my crystal in my hand as I turned to the News once more. I heard that a plane was shot down in Pennsylvania. My husband was out on a job and I had no way of getting ahold of him and did not know where the job was only that it was a few hours away. My heart started to race again, wondering if he was anywhere near the crash and at that time there was not enough information to know much at all. With all the vibrations and the emotions that were being stirred up I could not trust or judge my own thoughts, or instincts. My mind was rushing to come up with ways to get in touch with my husband or know where he was.

I spent the morning making phone calls and pacing the apartment. Hoping I would get a phone call, saying, my husband is safe. This was not a time where "no news was good news' I needed to know.

It was now noon and it was time for Danial's lunch when I walked into the kitchen I heard a truck pull up and out came my husband, he was safe and he was home.

That day and for many months later the energy of the pain of the loss of that day was strong, someone with my sensitivity and gifts felt it everywhere. I held onto my crystal cleansing it daily as we mourned this day. Some families got closure but many did not but our memory remains.

Every year after that day the world remembers the tragedy of that day with a tribute and a memorial. For many this is a comfort and a way to get close to those they loss but for others such as me it was not. I remember this day every single day and the memorial just adds salt to the never healing wound.

On that day, every year I stay home, shut my shades lock my doors and do not turn the television on. I do not want to see it again. I do not want to relive that day. For the whole week, they have documentaries and theories of that Fateful day. I do not watch them. Everyone that knows me know that on September 11th do not call me or reach out to me in anyway just leave me be and they did except for one, she did not get that memo. Abagail. In 2009 I had no choice but to answer the phone my youngest Daughter Zoey was pregnant with her fourth child and was due any time now and I was always there for the births of my grandchildren, so although there still were a few weeks left I did not hesitate to answer the phone call that came in on that day from Zoey. "mom, I know this is not a good day for you but I am in labor and I need you to meet me at the hospital." I got up and ran to the shower got dressed and before I left the house I found my black bag and took out my crystal and put it in the pouch of my sweatshirt so it was close to me. I got in the car and turned the radio on without thinking and swiftly drove to the hospital. As I neared the hospital my thought was directed to the music on the radio. "You look wonderful tonight" by Eric Clapton was playing, I gasped and tears were running down my face as I remembered the last time I heard that song. Tony and I had gone out to a bar for some dancing and I was feeling down about me and Tony could not have that So he pulled me on the dance floor as he sang to the song "You look wonderful tonight" As I pulled into the parking lot of the hospital my mind got brought back to the task on hand, the voice of my daughter came over the phone. "mom, are you here yet I need you." "I am here honey just pulled in I am going to park and be right up, hold on Zoey, I love you sweetie." Zoey was right, Abagail was on her way, she was going to be born on the one day out of the year that I dreaded the most. September 11, 2009. And two hours later Abagail came in like a firecracker, I saw the big light overhead turn on and shake and a bright ball of light shoot through the room like a fireball. The next thing I heard changed that dark day for me. The beautiful cry of my granddaughter, Abagail.

The Chief

It was a beautiful sunny day in April, everything seemed alive that day as I walked off my porch to go to do a reading up the road. It was a simple card reading I had done many times. Although this was something I did from a young age I still got nervous for every reading only wanting to give my client the best information possible, it was not about the money so I kept my prices low $45. And I spent as long as they needed. It was my way of helping people and spreading love energy.

Since the reading was 2 blocks up the road I decided to just enjoy the weather and walk. Just as I stepped off the porch and onto my walk way a Eagle flew over and as I looked up I saw a feather float to the ground. At that very moment I did not acknowledge the feather I just kept walking.

When I got to the door to where I was doing the reading and started to knock I got this strong smell of burning sage and

I heard light drumming in my inner ear and images of owls, and a native American boy dress in regalia dancing in a circle around the fire. This took me back a little wondering what this all meant. I took a deep breath and the door opened, a young girl in her 20's answered the door. "Hello, I said, my name is Trish I am here to do a reading are you my client?" "Yes, I am" she said and welcomed me in. I went over to the table and put my stuff down and prepared my table with incense of my own. I noticed that the smell of burning sage did not come from anywhere in the apartment building, the other apartments were being remodeled at the time.

My client was young in her very early 20" s and she was a very quiet young lady. She sat straight in her chair with her hands together on her lap. I watched her as she shuffled the card, she closed her eyes and held the cards close to her chest as if she was praying on every shuffle, she then placed them gently in the 4 piles in front of me like I asked, not once looking up at me until she was done and had sat back in her chair with her hands nicely on her lap. When she looked at me I saw this sadness in her eyes and felt drawn to them, as I looked into her eyes I saw this vision of an Eagle flying in the sky in a circle and I smelt the burning sage again. I soon focused on the card and read her cards. There is more there must be this is so straight and narrow just telling the story of the girl and her boyfriend and daily life. Then I heard the drums again and the owl and other symbols I saw before I entered the apartment. I folded up the card right then and I put them in a pile in front of me, I looked at the girl and I said" This is not what you came here for is it?" she nodded no telling me I was right then looked do at her lap. I closed my eyes taking in all the vibrations I could and there was for two to three minutes only the sound of me taking in deep breaths and letting them out clearing and cleaning myself and raising my vibrations.

"Someone close to you is passing, aren't they? I see woman around him day and night singing and they are dressed in native American ceremonial garb' are you native American? Oh, yes I said I see a crown on your head telling me you're a princess is this true?" she replied that she was of her tribe. Then she spoke for the first time, "what does he want us to do? I told her of the sacred items he wanted by his side and some of his last wishes and the future of the tribe. She asked me if his passing was to be soon and I said "yes.". He was the Chief and in his passing a New Chief would be appointed and there was some controversy on that decision. The Chief was her Uncle as well and very much like a father. The love, respect and honor they had for each other was very strong, the energy came through on both ends. The Chief although not passed yet let me know exactly what he wanted around him when he passed and his last wishes. The Princess stayed with me talking and asking the Chief other questions for about an hour. When I felt, the session was over I got this strong feeling that I had to give the Princess a gift, so I excused myself for a few moments and ran home and picked up the feather that had greeted me just before the reading and brought it back and gave it to the Princess. She cried because she knew it was an honorable gift from her Uncle and Chief. After I left the princess I could not get this reading out of my head, I still felt connected, the chief was still with me. The reading had drained me so I decided to lay down and try and take a nap, I closed my eyes but was awakened by the sound of the drums and the drums were getting louder so I texted the Princess and I explained to her that she needed to get things together and for fill the Chiefs last wishes for the time was getting closer for his passing. I promised the Princess that if I knew when he would pass to let her know. It had been 4 hours since She left, and the drums got not only louder but faster I knew it was time so I called the Princess, she did not answer so I texted her hoping she would receive my message. That was 2pm, The drums went silent, my text notification went off, "It is with sadness our Chief has crossed."

A few weeks later at the Mother's Day pow Wow they

honored his passing and a new Chief was chosen. The young boy I saw the day of the reading was dancing in full regalia around the circle of fire and as I looked up in the sky I saw an Eagle so majestically soaring around the circle. The sweat smell of sage in the air. At that moment, I felt tingles through my body and tears ran down my face. There was peace.

"Death - the last sleep?
No, it's the final awakening"
-Sir Walter Scott, 1771-1832
Author and Poet

Getting Ready

Through these years of my growing I have learned so much more about life and death than the average person of this earth. I have experienced life in such a way that it has given me a face value experience on life. Most people go through life guessing or having faith in something that they do not have any physical proof exists but they believe it like it is the only hope or only way. Their faith and upbringing has taught them the barriers of their beliefs and they cannot see beyond them. By doing this some people have a hard time understanding life after death or the concept of reincarnation even death itself. Their beliefs mainstream them which makes contact with the afterlife or the concept of Life and Death harder to comprehend. They fear the afterlife; spirits are not viewed as love energy. They are taught to fear the dead. In some cases, believe that spirits can cause physical harm. What if you let go of that for just a moment and see things like I do? what would you see? How would you feel?

I see people without their masks. I was never mainstreamed to believe that this life was built on a religious belief system. I was never clouded by the control of a higher power and taught to look for God in everything. That this God, he will make or break you. I grew up believing in the energies of the universe, in making your own destiny and that I am responsible for my own actions good or bad. If I live in the positive energies and not allow the negative than I will have a positive outcome in life. I believe that only I am responsible for my own actions and to own it. If I do bad than only I can change that action and only I am responsible for it... I believe in Karma good or bad and I take it seriously I do not use it as a threat because I do not have to. A higher power is not going to grant my wishes. A God does not give me what I can handle. Creating love energy and living in the positive along with the belief because if you think you cannot do something or something will never happen it will not. I work towards the positive. Dreams have been made by believing it will. I have free will in life, I make my choices. I create my destiny.

Life to me is never ending that's why it is called the circle of life. life, death, and rebirth. We are born and given life, a body, air to breath, at death, we shed our physical body, we release all physical limitations and become weightless and free. And rebirth we are reborn to a new life of our choosing.

Soon you realize that you are apart from the physical limitations of the body your soul feels joy and a feeling of relief from all the illness and pain they experienced in their physical body.

The body and mind are the hardest to let go upon death. The mind and body are part of the human experience that we are in that makes us a living entity. They will fight to stay connected. It is difficult to accept that life goes on because of the influences we were accustomed to in this human journey.

As the transition progresses the human mind realizes that life does continue and that life in the physical is like going to grade school, you are in this life to learn a lesson and if you fail, you must repeat this life again or you pass and graduate to the next lesson, each lifetime is an advancement of the soul. When the soul has learned all it is supposed to learn, sometimes being the lesson for someone else, when they have achieved a level of understanding of who they are, have many lifetimes as different beings, are open to other dimensions then they will become an "old Soul" and have achieved the level of spiritual wisdom and can choose to go on in other lifetime as a teacher, some people call this being "One with God", some feel this is an ascension to a" higher self"

People near their time of death have the capability to view the afterlife by moving in and out of the consciousness of other dimensions and seeing images of loved ones who have passed. I relate that part of the transition as "Nesting" getting ready.

Janise was my example of nesting. I knew Janise for 10 years before she passed. She was a remarkable woman and highly respected in my small town. I related so much to her and her story and she would tell me her story many, many times. "I was an orphan you know," she would say "never knew my family, I married the love of my life and we had our boys. I raised our boys most of their lives because I lost my husband at an early age and was left to raise our children." And she would go on telling me what it was like in that time in her life. She would go on and on about her life. I loved listening to her stories. He son and his wife live next door to me and decided to buy the house next to them and move Janise close to them. She was in her middle to late 80's and although she was quite active for her age her son felt that it was best she was close to them.

Every winter Janise would go out after the snow had fallen and start shoveling her sidewalks after her son and daughter in law left for work so one of my boys would go over and help her. We knew that Janise might feel offended so we came up with something to say to her that would make her not feel like she was incapable of her doing it by herself. and she would try and pay them for their services and again my boys told them they could not accept money from her because it was the right thing to do and they were not brought up that way. She would smile pat them on the back and say" Good boys you are, thank you."

A few years went by when I started noticing the grey mist around Janise. Daily she would take her dog for a walk by my house. She would stop right in front of my house and just stare at my house like she was waiting for me to come out and then turn and go back to her walking. I had been at the time babysitting my young grandchildren and could not go out and talk to her. This continued for a few months and as time went by she would stand looking at my house for longer periods of time. So one day when the kids were down for a nap I went out and stood on the porch so she would see me, she looked at me smile and took a deep breath, after a few days of that she finally would start talking to me, and all she would say is "I had a good life." I could see that the mist was getting bigger.

That weekend her son and daughter in law went away for the weekend and Janise was seen by my boys carrying stuff from her sons shed in the back yard of his house. So, they went over and asked her if they could help her and they proceeded to carry some possessions over to her house. "This vase was given to me by my love when he bought me roses for the first time, and this record was our song, and this tote hold my blanket and some of the pictures from when my husband was alive." We watched Janise as she caressed each item and spoke her memory's like there was nobody there and she was in the moment. The boys let her be trying not to disturb her moment. As they walked out the door they heard her say. "how much do I owe you boys for helping me?" "Nothing Janise, it is the right thing to do."

A week later I was on my way back from driving the kids to school and as I turned the corner I saw an ambulance blocking

"For all the wisdom of a lifetime
No one can ever tell, but whatever road you
Choose, I am right behind you win or lose.
Forever young"
-James Cregan,& Rod Stewart-

Forever Young

Today I still have Daniel in my life, 23 years at the time of this writing. Daniel is the only person that has ever accepted me completely. He has been my stability when I have needed it. He has been my partner and friend when I needed understanding and confidence in myself. Daniel sees me with open eyes and looks through the mask I must have to survive. I can be just the me that I am. Sometimes I do not know how I would have made it through without him and I bless each day that he has been. He believes in me more than I believed in myself. Some of my own children, after they met their partners could never see the me that I am.

I have spent my life helping those who ask me. I have had many people in and out of my life, some people not taking Me seriously and seeing that the person I am is real. Then I had the person who judges me and hates me with no real reason except for my beliefs and the gifts that I have and they always lurked around some corner watching me, waiting for any sign that I may transform into a green-faced, cackling Witch that will cast evil spells on them and cause destruction and harm to all who cross my path Bwahaaa. I did have a handful of people who know me and respect the person that I am and to this day still do.

I do know that it is hard to fully acknowledge and understand all that I am, the concept goes way beyond the box that they are in. To them I am fear and yet I am all that they have ever wanted to be. They have not realized that Fear is one of the most powerful emotions and creates one of the most powerful energies in the universe. Fear closes us off to our higher consciousness and the abilities like mine that are in all of us and only the individual can overcome fear and once done will open you up to the world in which I live in.

I have learned all about me through my lifetime here. Many times, I have questioned myself, especially in experiences when it is close and personal but in time I have been validated. Each experience teaches me a little bit more about myself and about life and the lessons I am supposed to learn while in this human earthly experience living the fast track as my soul attends and advances in the Earthly School of life. Each reincarnation teaches our soul what it needs to advance, some call it ascending to God. Here we have free will so our path and lessons become harder to reach and we can veer off our life course. In my life, each day of it has shown me my purpose for reincarnating into this life, Each day and event.

Our son Daniel3 graduated June 9, 2017 from High School and will be going off to College to achieve his dreams and passion. Through the course of events of the days leading up to his graduation and a few weeks after gave me so much validation and awareness of the me that I am in my own life.

Through a few stories in this book you have learned that

Daniel 3 had experienced the loss of his Uncle who was his Godfather and best friend in 2011 and his only Grandmother in 2015. They were very special to Daniel3 and all they talked about was how they wanted Daniel3 to be a success and they looked forward for him to get his diploma go to the college of his choice and play football. Daniel3's Uncles last words to him was that he wanted Daniel3 to grow up and be a respectful and successful young man. He told him he wished for him to go to the college of his choice and he would help him get there.

Wednesday of that week of graduation Daniel 3 came home with his cap and gown, he handed me his cap and said "Mom we are allowed to put a picture inside our cap and I want Uncle David and Nanny with me, so can you find me a picture that can go in my cap." I knew then they had found their way to be with Daniel3 on his important day. So, I found a picture and made a small oval frame in Daniel3 school colors and place it snuggly in his cap.

Doris, Daniel3's grandmothers biggest wish was to be able to see Daniel3 walk on Graduation day and the be there on moving day of college. She did not care what college Daniel3 attended she just wanted him to college.

Doris and I had talked about Daniel3 and getting pictures with him in his cap and gown and the graduation party afterword's. Doris was the Queen of party planning. I have never been a party organizer or hostess. I never opened my home up to outside people because of all the judgement so this alone was a big thing for me and to do this right I had big shoes to fill.

The week of graduation was just emotional. Just the Idea of Daniel3 graduating was hard enough, the thought of it was bringing me to tears but Doris let me know she was there and this woman who had always kept me on the sideline helped me plan this party. I could hear her voice as she whispered things in my ear. From the menu to the invitations. The next morning, I was awakened by a butterfly in my room fluttering around my head I had no idea how the butterfly got into my house and into my room and I never detected it. At that point I just knew, and did not take a second to question it, so I got up made coffee and Sat in my chair looking out the big living room window that looks out over the mountains and there right on my windowsill sat a beautiful cardinal looking right in at me." Hello David, and thank you for getting me up Doris I said allowed. Surprisingly enough the cardinal and the butterfly stayed around for the next few days.

Even if your reading this book and just do not buy into my experiences, you would have to agree that even the mere thought of the presence of a past love one would calm you down and it did. It just so happened that night was the beginning of craziness. Daniel3s father became ill that night and I was left with doing most the party by myself. How I managed it was a miracle within itself.

The Graduation ceremony was wonderful. We were such proud parents. My mind kept thinking about Doris and David. All day I felt them with me.

As the music played and Daniel3's name was called while he walked down the aisle to join his classmates I could not help picturing the pictures that were under Daniel3's graduation cap of his Uncle and his Grandmother and a ticket each to his graduation ceremony. When the Chorus sang as the orchestra played the song that was done at David graduation "forever Young" by Rod Stewart. We cried and we knew then that Doris and David had found their way to be there.

"Children are the anchors that hold a mother to life"
-American Baby Magazine-

The Mothers call in the night

The graduation party went off without a hitch. Daniel was still very ill and could not stay up for the whole party. He tried mingling with the guests and being a host to our son's friends and parents but it got the best of him and he had to call it a day, excuse himself and go lay down. The party continued for many more hours as Daniel slept, waking to either the chills and goose bumps or his cloths drenched in sweat.

The Tylenol and herbals I had been giving him seemed to help some but it did not seem to be getting him better. It was Saturday night so I made a mental note that Monday he would go to the doctors, hoping that tomorrow he would be himself again, after all this is the longest Daniel had ever been sick with no real improvement.

Sunday came and Daniel got up and seemed a little better but that was a momentary thought because within an hour of sitting on the porch with friends in 85* weather Daniel asked me for a jacket he was so cold he had goose bumps. Back to bed Daniel.

As the day passed it seemed Daniel started getting worse I could now see it in his color. He had this grey chalky color I have seen way too many times and it scared me. Daniel would not allow me to take him to the ER, he was still insisting that it was just a reoccurrence of his previous condition that can lay dormant. I kept giving him his herbals anxious for Monday to come so I could get him to his doctor and we could turn this around, get him on the upswing to better. That night Daniel woke saying he had heard his mother's voice calling his name and she had woken him up from a deep sleep. I knew what he was telling me really happened because when I walked into Daniel room I got a whiff of Doris's cologne. Daniel needed to get to the doctors this was something serious.

I got Daniel right in to see the doctor where their concerns alerted them to take blood work not only from one side of his body but both, sent him home without any prescription and the promise to call within 48 hours with results. Early the next morning they call and inform us that Daniel has a blood bacterial infection and would need to be place in the hospital A.S.A.P. they were calling the hospital and the hospital will be calling us back when a room was ready.

The day went by slowly as we waited and waited for us to get the go ahead to go to the hospital. The hospital was a hour and a half away and I could see Daniel getting worse with every hour. Finally, at 6:30 pm that evening the hospital called and told us to come up. I got Daniel in the truck and headed out. As I was driving I kept talking to Daniel to keep him awake but he kept slipping in and out, As I looked over at him I started to see a mist around him. The mist I see when a transition is beginning. Daniel was sick and he was starting to die. I closed my eyes for a second took a deep breath, asked for all the lights to be green and put my foot on the gas. All the lights were green as I raced my way to the hospital trying not to panic knowing time was running out. I made it to the hospital in record time, not giving how much time incase Daniel read this book. (*giggle, giggle*)... I can hear him now "you went how fast in my new truck? You could have wrecked my truck and killed us all." He will not see the validity in that.

The hospital was huge and they only gave us room a number to report to. Rm 636. As we got to the entrance of the hospital Daniel could not go any farther and there was no one there in the lobby to help us and I had no idea where to go, so I left Daniel in a chair in the lobby as I went in search for someone or an elevator. ¾ of the way down the long corridor I found the elevator, so I went back put Daniel in a wheel chair and pushed this 6ft 10 400lb limp man down the long corridor into the elevator to the 6th floor. We get to the desk at the end of the hall and they say "No Mrs. Avery, they changed your room you are now on the 3rd floor room 342 go down this hall to the elevator." I abruptly and sharply said I know where the elevator is how do you think I got here" Trying to keep it together I pushed him back down the corridor to the elevator to the third floor, down the long hall to the desk. A cheerful nurse comes around the corner and say to us," are you our incubation? From the emergency room?" I told her that we were not and that we were told to come to the hospital we had been waiting all day and were supposed to come to room 636, she interrupts me and say "well you are on the wrong floor" at this point I am at the end of my line here, I roll my eyes take a deep breath and say "no, if you had let me finish I was going to tell you they changed his room and sent us to this floor for rm 342" she gives me a funny look as she types in the room, She looks at me and says "I am sorry but that room is taken." "Daniel is on the 6th floor. Ok I do not think I need to explain to you how I felt at that moment. Daniel is limp I have just gone on a wild goose chase because no one knew anything in this hospital, the grey mist is extending farther out of Daniel. Just at the moment of total outburst. A male nurse gets up from behind the desk and says

I know where he is supposed to go "follow me" he says. I was relieved that someone finally knew where we were to be. With a duffle bag on one shoulder, pocket book flung over the other and Daniel in a wheel chair I followed this tall muscular male nurse down another long corridor as we stopped to adjust the duffle bag that kept falling off my shoulder. (me just for info. 145lbs, 5'3) I shook my head and cursed him under my breath. Could he not even just take a bag from me? This man was stocky and about 6ft tall, it would be nothing for him to push Daniel. It is his job he should be used to it. Not to mention It is the right thing to do.

We walked down another long corridor, stopping many times to adjust the duffle bag that I was carrying over my shoulder that every few steps would slip off my shoulder and rub against the wheel chair making it harder to push. The nurse got us to our room. Daniel was hunched over in the wheel chair and his complexion was very grey. Two nurses came in and took his vitals the next thing I knew is I was sitting in a chair in the corner of the room and first responders were packing Daniel with Ice to get his temperature down. Daniel had bacteria in his blood and it was shutting down his organs, he was sepsis and going into shock. I spent the night by his side wondering if I was going to lose Daniel. Did his mother come the other night because she was there to greet him, or just to warn us that Daniel needed to go to the Doctor because this was serious. I was in a fog, so much out of touch of the me that I am. I couldn't feel me, or the knowing I always had. I was normal as most people would perceive it. My gifts were frozen I felt so alone and so unsure as to what would be next. This man was the only person I did not have to hide from, or explain to. I never thought that Daniel would not be here I always thought that I would go first. I did not realize till that moment how much I needed Daniel. Would I be able to continue to be me? He was the support of me being open to who I am. He is the support of me telling my story. To him I am not weird or strange, I am not evil or dark. Daniel was not just my partner, the father to my son and my best friend. Daniel saw me and encourages me to be me. I sat there wondering, if I would be me if I lost Daniel or if I would go back into hiding?

Daniel stayed in the hospital for a week and I drove an hour and a half back and forth daily. My gifts remained frozen, this was a feeling and a normal I was never used to and it rocked my core. My anxiety was peeked and my balance off.

Daniel went into the hospital on a Tuesday, that Friday I knew I had to get me back, I knew all this stress and being over tired was clouding me and clogging my chakras I knew what I needed to do. When I returned home, Thursday might I drank a bottle of water to flush my system then prepared a nice cup of Jasmine tea. Jasmine is a calming herb, it sooths your spirit the moment you smell the brew tea. I drink it to help calm the stress of the day. I took a few rescue remedy anti stress soft lozenges, took a deep breath and sat back in my soft chair in the dark silence of my Livingroom.

How could I not know the outcome? How could I not see or feel? I always have been able to. This was too close, was I only able to use my abilities to help others and not for my own life? I needed to know and feel that Daniel was going to be ok. Not being able to have my intuition and my knowing is like not being able to breathe and I feel like I am gasping for air. Then I had that moment, you know that moment when it all come clear. I went into my room and grabbed my crystal. I lay flat on my back and passed the crystal over my body. I rubbed it on my forehead where my third eye is located. I searched my Cd's and IPod for my chakra meditation and took 30 minutes and cleared and opened my chakras. I released all my blocks that were created through the stress of the past 2 weeks and the anxiety. Normally I would take such steps and precautions to not create these blocks to begin with but even the best of us have these super-being moments when we think "not me, I am above that." "after all I have been doing this every day one or two days missed will not hurt." Well? It was not 1 or 2 days it was 2 weeks and it did hurt, it shut me down and through me way off kilter. Not keeping up with it was like my kryptonite. Going in and out of the hospital without my shields with all the emotions and energies surrounding that place made everything much worse.

Daniel was doing better and they were figuring out how to heal him so I took that day to clear myself, recharge and gain my strength so that I could regain me. Amazingly enough it did the trick. The next day I was back to me and ready to help Daniel get him back.

A few days later Daniel came home. It was going to be a few weeks for recovery but we will do it. This health experience for Daniel was a spiritual learning for him as well, it opened doors for him and his lessons came rushing in. For him it was an awakening like one may have in a near death experience.

"Heal the hurt,
Don't hide the pain"
                    -Melanie Koulouris-

The Addiction;
A message to my father

I met Patrick 11 years ago, when he was in his early 20" s. He was the nephew of someone very close to me named Joseph, who became my yin-and-yang of my life.

Patrick was a rough and tough kind of guy who lived life on the edge. He was an athlete in high school but always with the bad boy attitude. I did not know much about his younger years except what he had told me and stuff that was told underneath other family members stories.

Patrick was the oldest of two boys they lived in the middle of inner city New York where walking to the corner was dangerous. Their parents had divorced and their father had done time in jail, so Patrick did not have a father in his life for a few years.

Patrick's young life was rough growing up in the city.

Patrick had to learned to survive like any other kid brought up in the heart of city life where row homes were common place and drugs and violence filled the streets. By the time, Patrick was in his early 20's he was a father and being a father meant everything to Patrick. Patrick worked hard every day to provide for his son and girlfriend Tiffany. He established a trade that payed him a high union wage. Like any trade there were the normal ups and downs.

When I met Patrick through Joseph he was an aggressively happy guy that loved to have a good time. He seemed genuinely happy to meet me and thrilled that I was a part of his uncle's life. He was very curious about me and my abilities but also a skeptic. He wanted me to contact his grandmother and he wanted to hear from her, to know if she was ok and to tell her he loved her and he missed her so much. His grandmother had died when Patrick was a young boy and it was a great loss to him.

Any medium can tell you that talking to spirits is not a dial up service where a medium will say "Hello, grandma, Patrick is here and wants to chat." Contacting is more on the spirit than the medium and most mediums are not always open up on call either. Mediums shut themselves down in the outside world, if they did not do that then not only would the medium be drained all the time but it would drive them to the looney bin. Needless to say, I did not tune into his grandma. Patrick's opinion of me changed at that moment. I felt bad for that but I could not lie to him, for it would have been easy, I told him the truth that I could not at that time and took his disappointment in me.

Patrick although he was a happy guy on the outside I could see he was troubling on the inside and searching so hard for something. He loved his music and often found his solace in the music he listened to. The words spoke to him. I would see Patrick at family gatherings and he was full of love for family. He loved celebrating and loved the party, often a little too much but he always had a bright smile and would often share his love for music by singing to the crowd, but I knew there was something behind that, something that was deep down I could see it in his eyes and feel it in his energy. He felt lost.

Tiffany and Patrick split after a few years and Patrick's son stayed with Tiffany and that left Patrick with weekend visitations. He felt the loss of his son every day. This was a feeling he never wanted his son to have to feel, a feeling Patrick knew all too well having been separated from his father in his younger years. This was another obstacle in Patrick's life and weighed heavily on him. This man who came across as tough on the outside and aggressively happy in the presence of others, was troubled and sensitive. He did not know his place in this world and on many occasions asked me what I thought his purpose was. His father at this time was back in his life and I believe he asked his father the same question because when they would come to visit Patrick's dad would sit for hours preaching the bible and Gods word to him and his brother. As I watched them I could see Patrick brighten up like he was finding hope in his father's words, I do not know if it was the words of the bible or just the fact that it was his father who was preaching it to him. I would love to say both because any connection to one's spirituality is a good thing, but the energy I saw and felt at those moments were his love for his father and these times he got his undivided attention even if he shared those moments with his brother it was still a moment very special to Patrick.

Somehow Patrick's search for finding where he belonged and the constant struggles along the way led him to the dark place of addiction. Alcohol and drugs.

We never really truly know what brings someone down that road, it is a personal one and mostly masked by our outer image. We could say that Patrick's rough life and struggles led him to drugs and alcohol and I do believe it was part of it. I believe he felt by escaping he was somehow how finding his place, that place where he belonged. This place he was looking for was indescribable for him. I know this because I saw this same lost person in his uncle Joseph. Joseph and I talked about it on many occasions, they both had good jobs and adventures in their life, they had people who loved them dearly but they were always missing something and searching for that place where they belonged. Patrick went in and out of rehab sometimes staying clean for years. He had the love and support from all his family without judgement.

One night in early June I was woken by a whisper in my ear and a pressure on my bed. I sat up and there in front of me was Patrick. I was barely awake and my sight and senses were not awake yet. I looked at the clock and it was just past midnight. Not fully aware I said Patrick what are you doing here and how did you get here in my room? Just as I was saying it I realize Patrick was not in human, physical form he was in spirit. He said to me that he needed help he did not know where he was or how he got there and needed to find his way home. I asked him to give me details and all he could show me was street lights and he was gone. I laid back down and went back to sleep thinking I was in a dream, because a few years prior I had had a dream like that about Patrick and people thought I was crazy because Patrick was home with his father the night of the dream.

The next morning, I get a knock on my door from Joseph, he was in tears of disbelief, Patrick was found dead on a street corner in New York City in an area he had never been known to be because it was an area just driving through could get you killed. Patrick was just 34 yrs. old and he died of an overdose. My heart sank and all I could do is hold Joseph why he cried. His family was very religious and for the last part of the 11 years of Joseph being in my life they had judged me and hated me for who I was and what I believed. The ironic part of that, so did Patrick. Telling them of what had happened the night prior would have not made thing better nor would it have been a comfort to them so I chose to keep it to myself. I also know grief and how telling them would give them someone to blame, like I could have saved him in some way. My experience would not make anyone any better. I was pretty much not welcome at the funeral services; Josephs family was enraged at the fact that Joseph found himself consoled with me at this time. I did not go to the services but although the family had such dislike for me I still felt sympathy for them and lit a candle for Patrick and his family.

Until their judgement of me and before they found out through Joseph what they called my deep dark secrets that they felt were incriminating Joseph, before all that, our families were one.

The loss was devastating to the family that did everything to heal this broken soul and every one of them felt the weight of some guilt they thought contributed to Patrick's passing.

Patrick came to me twice after that. I had to explain to him where he was and what had happened. He expressed his love for his father and family especially his son. He said he was with his grandmother and other loved ones that had passed. He was worried about his father and his step mother because they were taking his passing very hard. He wanted his father to hold on to his faith because it was what made him strong and that he wanted his father to take care of his son for him, not to let him go down this road, do not hide what Patrick had done from his son for there is a lesson in it. Tell him his dad is always with him and loves him purely. Read to him your scriptures for the words are universal and coming from you dad is where the love is.

Rest in peace Patrick.

The question that I am sure that is wandering around in your head is that If Patrick did not like me in life why would he come to me in death?

In simple form: because he knew he could. He might have feared me and judged me in human life but in spirit he knew he could get me his message, with me his soul could find direction. He knew not fear which gave him judgement. I was his beacon in both worlds.

Our earthly humanness has connected us to our here and now. Which gives us our vessel for our soul which combined gives us human life. Human life, upon it's connection, gives us free will, and all human thought and emotions; fear, anger, happy, sad and so on. When Patrick's soul left his human vessel, and entered spirit it released all human emotions and soon after recognizes the spirit world and the source in which it came. So, his dislike for me had no validity in the spirit world. I was his messenger and his guide.

Joseph like I said earlier was my yin and yang in life because at times Joseph understood who I was and my beliefs because I never kept that from him and there was part of me he could accept but part of me he could not and at times would in a rage or an insecure moment in his life where he himself felt judged, not by me but by others and would lash out at me. He would throw in my face the person I am and try make me seem like a horrible person and he would speak that to all who would listen. Well us living in a small town where they felt we were transient's because we were not born and raised in this town, stirred things up for me, to the point that sitting in the bleachers at my son's football game watching him got glares from other town people hoping they would get a glimpse of me casting spells on unsuspecting people or even players to get an advantage in the game.

I found this amusing at best and knew that instead of being that quiet mysterious type I needed to start mingling and getting to know more people and more importantly get to know me. It did take some time but soon people did not see me as a threat any longer because I had nothing to hide. With this I ended up getting more clients at times more than I could handle.

Joseph loved me very much and he was a big part of our

lives but he too always felt that he did not know where he belonged. Not matter how happy he was and how hard he tried he couldn't figure it out. He too has an addiction, not to drugs but to alcohol, that ever since he ran from me has increased and hope one day soon he finds that missing place in his life because one thing I know about this man is that through the 11 years I have known him I have noticed he has the gift of spirit just like me.

Patrick - from the moment I met you I saw the little boy in you, I saw your soul, the lost boy behind the addiction, and behind the man. He is love...

"cause it is not like you, to walk away in a middle of a song. Your beautiful Song, Your absolutely beautiful Song"

Why ;by Rascal Flatts

The Me that I am

As my story, has unfolded with little fractions of it that have impacted my life are put into words for all to read it makes me wonder why me? I defy all statistics. The lack of parental guidance, living through rejection, neglect and abuse, heart ache, being misunderstood. How did I survive those younger years where I was just a toddler? A mother who had no motherly skills just addictions. The things I went through in life should have caused major trauma in my life, I should be according to, science, public opinion and doctors research one messed up woman. But yet I sit here addiction free, sober no anxiety issues or anger, writing this book. My mother did not nurture and I was in foster home after foster home at the age of 4 with no real stable life there as well.

How did I learn how to take care of my older siblings in that closest? I do not remember before the age of 3 so I could not tell you those first 2 years of my life, it is like I remember waking up in a closet and that is where my life began.

I look around at my grandchildren today and remember the youngest ones just a few years back and them learning to walk and potty - training them. At those ages, there was no way that they could have been me at 3. I do remember still being in a diaper when I was put in my first foster home and a crib that to me was not comforting because I had never known a crib before. Not being in the ripped yellow dress I had worn most of the time and wearing pants for the first time. Pants? that too was new to me. The question remains, how did I learn to be me? And why am I not a statistic. I have raised to date 4 children and am totally in love with my 13 grandchildren. How did I learn nurturing? How did I learn to be a mother?

My abilities have stayed with me all my life and have been my survival through all the years. I cannot say I always listened to them but who does all the time. Sometimes you just need a little bit of a challenge and to do things the hard way. If you do not get your heart broken then how do you know you love? if you do not fall and get hurt, then how do you know pain.? If you're not wrong, then how do you learn? Who I have been has been me. My abilities were not strange to me, it was others that made me strange. Are we not all born the same way? Are we not all newly born with a clean slate and must learn and grow.?

So, again. How did I learn to be me? I didn't I just was and "I am that I am" (*Exodus: 3:14)* and I slipped "Through the Cracks"

The Reflection of the Soul

As I look into the mirror I see the face and body of a Woman, of a mother and a grandmother. I see what people see when they look at me. I close my eyes and look within. I feel the woman who is standing there. I know her. I see her and I hear her.

I take a deep breath in, like I am breathing in the universe. I feel new and refreshed, comforting and peaceful. Then I exhale and breathe out all the unbalance, the hurt and insecurities that have trapped themselves inside of me. Life has been tough and the world is changing in such a way that you cannot recognize the real person. What is on the outside is not what is on the inside. Our soul is trapped inside and dogma is taking control.

I open my eyes and look at myself in the mirror once again. "What do people see when they look at me?", I wonder. Do they know me? The reflection in the mirror even to me doesn't look like the woman that I know inside. It is hard to wonder sometimes about that woman in the mirror, I do not feel like her, but I am her.

I look around me at the people in my life and the family that I built. Each relationship is different and each person sees something else the others do not, like I am 10 different people with the same name and face. Do they see only what they need to see?

I don't have the experience of true family life, I did not grow up that way. I wasn't born to a happy family and adorned with pretty bows and pink dresses. I didn't come home to smiling faces of family and friends and laid in a nursery with mobiles and frills. I was born to a single mother who knew only a rough side of life. Her life was filled with darkness and bad choices and repeated mistakes. She left me not knowing what it is like to be loved by a mother or a father, so I do not know how my love feels to my children or how it feels to my child to have a mother. This mother thing was all new to me upon the birth of my first child, and yet I never asked how I was going to do it, how I was going to be that person, how I was going to "mother", I just did.

I grew up with brothers who view me now as a stranger because somehow that world changed and not being blood made a difference. Along the way, I was able to find my bloodline of brothers and sisters, nieces and nephews even my own twin sister, whose life I would love to be a part of, but they see me as the secret inside the Pandora's box and they are so afraid to see what's inside, afraid to see me. The truth of who I am is unbearable to them because then their life, their reality would change. I cannot fit into their fairytale that they chose to be their reality. I am their Pandora's box.

I grew up going from home to home never establishing what most people call "real roots', till finally at the age of fifteen I decided it was time to do this my way. Through my childhood, I was a product of abuse, neglect and abandonment and even rape. The inside of my locked closet was a common and familiar place at night (instead of what most people would have is a babysitter), the closet was my babysitter. It was my safe place. The place that among the darkness where a world of adventure and beautiful things were imagined and secrets told. I learned then how to astral travel not knowing at a young age what it was called it was just something I did to see the world and pass the time inside my locked closet.

When I had an opportunity to be part of a "family", it was cut short do to the death of an infant child and I became a witness to her death. That was the first and last real experience of a family and my first time seeing the soul begin to depart, only briefly though, I was young and not allowed in the hospital room I watched it from a television screen outside the intensive care unit. It was then I knew I was different. I felt different. That was the beginning of who I am.

A few years later when great grandpa called my name. I waved to him as his soul lifted away knowing he was on his next great adventure as his body lay peaceful in his bed. I looked in his mirror wondering if I would see him floating and all I saw was me. It would not be till my older years that I would discover that the reflection in the mirror only reveals a mask for the soul.

As they say that the eyes are the key to the soul and to look deep within them will reveal the secrets of many lifetimes. This statement remains true and can be proven with one deep look into one's eyes. In those eyes lies truth and many lifetimes of emotion. It is then that you can see the soul and uncover the true person inside the costume we call the body.

In today's world, we look at people as we do when we look in the mirror. We look at the costume and the reflection and avoid the eyes. We do not see or hear the soul. As a young child, I knew that I could see the soul and I could hear its whisper. I could feel the pain that was deep within, the things that others could not because they were to busy looking at the reflection in the mirror. Before the world changed love was found in a look into someone's eyes from across the room, anger and pain noticed without words. Entering a room with your eyes closed, you could hear the whispers of the soul and when you opened your eyes and looked into others, you would know the whispers were right. I was not so different then. Today we are so wrapped up in dogma we forget to look with in. We forget that we are a soul with a body that hides all our secrets and all our past and many lifetimes. We look up to God for answers, we look up to God to find who we are and spend a life time doing it looking for our life purpose. We forget to look within, to stare deeply into that mirror, past the mask to the soul, to the place that holds our beginning and our ending. We forget to open ourselves up to all possibilities, to soar outside the box, to be God-like and not *controlled or crippled* by God. We forget that Religion should be a source of teaching, not a tool of control and judgment. We forget to use Religion in combination with our inner soul and to look with in, to use your abilities and take off the mask so we can look past the reflection in the mirror and see the person that stands in front of the mirror. We need to look to the soul and unchain it from the dogma of the world that has changed, feel the person who is standing there. Listen to the whisper, ask "What do people see when they look at me?"

Appendix

Chakras

Are center points in our body that energy flows through. When working with your natural abilities it is important to keep the Chakras open and spinning Think of a telephone pole of electrical line. The energy flows through free and clear but if there is a knot in the line or a break it stops the connection. The Chakras work the same way and when maintained can influence spiritual and emotional expression. I use 12 of them regularly.

I will start with the first chakra and move upward to the twelfth.

First: Red-Root -base of the spine- grounds- confidence, intuition, survival. Is blocked by Fear.

Second: Orange - lower abdomen- sacral-confidence and desire, enthusiasm, sensuality, passion. Is blocked by Guilt.

Third: Yellow-between navel and sternum-solar plexus-inspiration, personal energy, extroversion, sharpness, growth, power- Is blocked by shame.

Fourth: Green - center of chest-heart- compassion, understanding, love devotion. Is blocked by Grief.

Fifth: Blue- throat-calm, confident, clear communication, assurance, clarity, security. Is blocked by Lies.

Sixth: Indigo-forehead between eyebrows-third-eye, consciousness, vision, balance, visualization, intuition. is blocked by illusions.

Seventh: Violet-top of head-crown-transcendence- release, free thought, spirituality. Is blocked by indecisiveness and depression.

Eighth: Seafoam green- 12in above the body-last of human chakras-energy center of divine love, understanding of spiritual Identity.

Ninth: Blue green - few feet above head- Soul blueprint, abilities learned in all lifetimes, aides in soul merge.

Tenth: Pearl white- eight to ten feet above the crown-aligns to the solar system, Divine Creativity, synchronicity. aligns with the chakras below the feet.

Eleventh: Pink Orange - located outside the human body, accessible through the hands and feet - travel beyond the limits of time. Path to the soul, advanced spiritual skills, teleportation, telekinesis, balances humanity.

Twelfth: Shimmering Gold - connection to the cosmos, connection to the monadic level of divinity. Ascension energy, and helps all chakras accelerate faster than light.

Much of this information can be found at; I highly encourage you to check these sources and others out to help you on your journey.
wisdomsdoor.com
theawakenedstate.net
Chakras for beginners; by David Pond
New Chakra healing; activate your 32 energy centers; by Cyndi Dale

Shielding

I learned many years ago, that every day shielding is part of survival. Every person creates an energy which can be good or harmful to themselves and others. For someone who is open like myself it can shut them down.

Have you ever walked in a friend's house after they had an argument and you knew right away, you could feel it even without the people being in the room?

Have you ever been around someone that just by their very presence you felt agitated?

These are just a few examples where shielding can be a great benefit. These energies can cause illness and mood-swings in you just by being in the presence of these energies.

Going to the mall at holiday time, the tension makes me moody, dizzy, and drains me. I am known to cover my solar plexus so not to absorb the chaos.

Some of the things I do:

To my home: Smudge with sage daily and after someone enters my home after they leave.

I surround my house with protective light (white or blue) and visualize mirrors facing out of my home so when someone feels they want to verbally, mentally or spiritually attack me it reflects back at them.

I also do daily affirmations of positive energy.

I have also use crystals to absorb energy as well as salt lamps (love them) I carry my 7crystal with me at all times.

At night, I surround myself with white light while sleeping.

I have also used diluted sea salt in a spray bottle and spray corners of my home and car.

Jewelry is also a very important protection for me but because of the beauty of my crystal and emblems I wear as well as the energy it gives off people want to touch it. People that is a number 1 NO! NO! do not touch someone's jewelry especially without permission.

There are many other shielding and groundings out there for you to try and whether we are on the same path or not keep in mind the universe is full of energy and we are affected by it.

Ground to your life source, Mother Earth.

Food for thought: magic, prayer, and other forms of divination cannot flow to and from when chaos exists.

- Namaste-

In Memory, Of

Vicky, my dearest of friends - my time with you was full of girlish laughs and rewarding memories. I will always remember our time. 1959-2006

David - The lessons you taught us, your adventures and your strength to be who you wanted to be. Your love and compassion is greatly missed. It is Ironic that today the finishing of the book Aug 13, 2017 marks 6 years since we said "We will see you again" (1972-2011)

Doris - To me you were a great teacher, so full of love and compassion for all you would meet. You challenged me in many ways and as I held your hand when you journeyed on I could not help but think about how different the world would be, but am reminded every day of the blessing your strength, and values have impacted my life." I loved you then and love you still" (1946-2015)

To all those who's stories I wrote about. Your presence in my life has been a great part of my journey to today, even if the meeting was a brief one. I will always remember you for the part you had in my lessons on Earth. Till we meet again I am reminded once again that "Love never Dies"

Printed in the United States
By Bookmasters